PERSONALITY

PERSONALITY
A PICK-ME-UP GUIDE

BALKRISHNA PANDAY

PARTRIDGE
A Penguin Random House Company

ISBN: Hardcover   978-1-4828-1246-6
               Softcover   978-1-4828-1244-2
               Ebook   978-1-4828-1245-9

Queries and clarifications
desired, welcome: bkpanday32@gmail.com.

To order additional copies of this book, contact
Partridge India
000 800 10062 62
www.partridgepublishing.com/india
orders.india@partridgepublishing.com

CONTENTS

FOREWORD

I have been an avid reader of spiritual articles published in national dailies over a long time. The deep interest resulted in a collection of clippings published during a span of fifteen to twenty years.

The massive collection of articles was sorted out, grouped and arranged topically for presentation. The matter was studied in depth for continuity and maintenance of readers' interest in heavy-weight intellectual and philosophical content. Added on were relevant comments and critique where needed. The basket of knowledge is thus presented with suitable additions and alterations.

The subjects covered are inclusive of Knowledge, as it is available and limitations thereof. '*Anubhava*' (Experience plus mental comprehension of a deeper meaning) as it forms the pith of Knowledge. Mind is explained as a guide for worldly affairs and the control it needs with the tool of practice. Resolve, without which no forward movement is possible. Ego, the cause of all that happens and the spoil-sport that it can be. Nothingness, explained as the resultant vacuum of whatever is material in the universe. Karma dealt with as the seed for, good, bad and neutrality with potential for positive or negative and oh yes, the rebirth, if so believed in. Love, it all depends, of the body or of the spirit. A path to super-consciousness has been indicated in simple terms.

The purpose is to look forward to a pick-me-up pragmatic spirituality guide as is gainful now to be applicable to development of individual personality and desirability of life as lived in modern times.

Balkrishna Panday

CHAPTER – 1

KNOWLEDGE

"Go placidly amid the noise and the haste, and remember what peace there may be in silence", is a quote from the famous document *Desiderata* by American mystic poet Max Ehrmann.

Knowledge as this one is the pith of wisdom of the wise, which cannot but be of the wise. Let us give credit and be obliged to the source of origin. All knowledgeable persons are not wise of their knowledge although they may speak the oft-repeated words of wisdom. There is a stream of thought process that helps the wise ones to arrive at nutshells of wisdom.

Talking of streams, writer Janine Gomes writes that sometimes we find, the streams of our lives can run into frozen winters. In an actual instance beneath the surface, in a little stream (the stream was only about four yards wide) the water in the waters ran deep. She mentions that Klemens Tilmann found a profound symbolism, the upper stream was in constant movement. Parts of the stream were frozen over and large areas of ice that had survived colder weather and had become covered by the energetic flow of the water above. But, the water flowing beneath the flat surfaces of ice was full of bubbles, dancing and vibrating.

The water of the stream sometimes encountered obstacles, and at other times flowed freely. Sometimes it ran in the opposite direction to the current only to later join the mainstream. All these different processes were observed by Tilmann. He was impressed by the water's obedience to its own essential being. Tilmann saw in this little stream a symbol of what all human life on this earth was meant to be. Human life to be attune with the phenomenon of nature. Lovely thought that indeed. Just suppose you were an adventure tourist with your group of friends negotiating the rapids of this stream on a raft guided by paddles. You would be experiencing a chilling thrill in the company of your social circle. Your overwhelming sentiment would be of conquering the obstacles of nature and their vehemence. This would be *experience* not *knowledge*.

The integral knowledge from the stream for the individual's *self* would be along the lines of earlier paragraph.

By contrast to the adventure, if one were sitting along the bank of the stream, enjoying the scene calmly and the similarity of nature and the way to live human life, meaning of the words, "Go placid," would dawn upon oneself as if a solution to a mathematical paradox, clarifying the concept of happiness, (call it '*Ananda*'). This solution may be ingrained deep. "*Shruti*" or scriptures of the philosophy of Hindu religion have tried to bring forth that experience which is based on immediate action-reaction with the world, is mentioned as '*Maya*'. This phenomenon is transitory and amenable to the consistent process of change.

That other part of this worldly *experience* with '*Maya*' which is steady, consistent, unlimited and reflects one's real nature in its rapport with one's soul is *knowledge*. It is in this knowledge that one picks up a moment of happiness, 'ananda', and one does not want to let go this moment. It is desired for all the time.

When you want 'ananda' (i.e. His grace) all the time, meditation comes in handy. In the year 2003 Nilanshu Ranjan writes that an enlightened being is an individual. The spiritual, enlightened and mystics do not want their faithful, their followers to adhere to any specific beliefs. They are actually taught to have a questioning mind. They are in fact trained to have an empty mind devoid of fleeting thoughts. The learning is by virtue of spoken or unspoken communication of a rationale leading towards reality, the truth.

Preoccupation with thoughts is bound to mislead the mind and pushes it in myriads of directions. Emptying of mind is not that difficult, as it appears to be. You just let the thoughts be, let them come and go as they may. One uses the emptiness resulting from care-free attitude to develop consciousness, awareness by one's inner self, an acuteness to understand and realize at a noble stratum, the reality, the truth. The truth would primarily relate to one's *individuality*. Individuality ought not to be erroneously confused with personality, as is likely. **The enlightened people** also called 'sadgurus' i.e. holy teachers, help the learners, the pupils, to discover their *individuality* which lies dormant, subdued, suppressed and unblossomed.

On account of suppressed *individuality* a very meagre percentage of our physical and mental capacities come into actual play in the societal field.

Ranjan writes that what we claim to know about *individuality* is nothing but personality. Personality is not *individuality*. Personality is not of much importance. Psychologically it may be of utmost importance but spiritually, personality has no value. Spiritually speaking, *individuality* is innermost and it has to be discovered and not invented because it is very much there. Individuality means not to borrow from others, not to be conditioned. Personality is the outcome of our conditionings. Personality is that which is thrust upon us, by parents, teachers, society etc.

That which exists is existential. Existentialism is a modern system of belief propounded by Jean Sartre in 1940s, in which the world is meaningless. Each person is alone and completely responsible for one's own action by which one makes own character.

Somewhat in this light Osho states that *individuality* is *existential.* In the ordinary course, a person with un-developed inner consciousness has no individuality, he has only a personality. Personality is the result of our conditioning by family and social environment. Only when individuality blossoms you become one with the whole (i.e. totality of universe). The experience of becoming the whole is of consciousness and the expression of it is through the body/mind. When one goes into deep meditation, one becomes absolutely silent; he is neither body nor mind. He is far above them. It is a stage of pure consciousness.

What obstructs the individuality to follow development of inner consciousness? Evil. Evil is the roadblock to *ananda,* pure incessant happiness. Bindu Chawla writes in 2005 "Any life of *sadhna* or devotion unleashes evil, so that the agenda for meditation becomes for us the war with evil before it is peace with *ananda.* The word evil has a simple meaning. It comes from the word German 'ubel', meaning 'ill'. The word 'diabolic', however, has a complicated etymology. It comes from the 'diaballein', from 'dia' meaning 'to throw', and 'ballein', meaning 'across'. Clearly, to throw away poison or negativity.

Given the nature of all illness, the wise have always recommended the killing of poison before the poison decides to kill. First, the nature of evil should be understood. Like the 10 heads of Ravana, evil, in the course of any kind of *sadhana* we undertake, not only rears its head mercilessly, but has unending resilience.

Second, evil is perennially connected to 'good'. They are two sides of the coin, for where there is good there is evil, masked. So it is difficult for an ordinary person to discriminate and avoid coming under its spell. Evil is created by The Void, the spiritual gap between man and God. As opposed to love (bhakti or devotion) which alone can fill this gap, the Void, ends up being powerful.

The void where evil resides results in a state of anxiety in the individual. Mukunda Goswami writes in 2004, anxiety is a bummer. When it strikes, some resort to counseling and others to drugs, legal and illegal, Distress is what nobody wants, like garbage in your bedroom.

Wished for or not, feelings of **quiet desperation**, call it depression, descend on us all, When it's a daily occurrence enduring for all one's waking hours, something drastic needs to be done. Switching on the tube, shopping, going to the movies, and bingeing on food or alcohol just don't get it, not long term anyway.

What we do and the people we see, most often affect us. Adages like Shaw's 'you are what you eat', and 'A man is known by the company he keeps reflect this.

It is a tenet of contemporary psychology that an individual's mental health is supported by having good social networks.

One successful way of curing a life of anxiety or depression is to alter its course by and by modelling oneself internally as well as externally upon the people one respects and regards high in esteem. Pick up their values and imbibe them step-by-step steadily. Notice and check-up when one fails. It is tedious, lifting oneself up from the morass but yes, it is possible. Anxiety and distress will shed piecemeal. By the time this chapter is over you shall have a very dear friend, close to your heart. Yes, **your intuition, your conscience**. Do rely upon your own opinion from within. Stick to it with rationale. The world around shall fall in line.

It is the void that is created between spirituality and the life when the uniformity, the oneness of the ultimate truth in all religions is lost in the maze of tenets of religion.

The follower of fundamentalism sticks to the strict observance of the tenets of religion as they happen to be understood or misunderstood. The agony of getting the tenets of own religion forced for acceptance upon the non-followers of those beliefs or mores, is transferred to the society for cracks therein and the vehemence thereof. The disease is equally spread amongst the expansionist followers of, be it Islam, Christianity and certain others too. Expansionism has in lap, violence of sorts, mild or strong. The one and the only remedy is to look to the ultimate truth which is Secular in all religions.

To be spiritual, I sincerely recommend deep breathing exercise. Close your eyes physically and from the world. Taste the peace of meditation. Remember God or the power that creates fate for you, in the peace of your closed eyes.

Chant in your mind, if you may, His name if you have or if one is accorded by you.

Here, this is an easy path under-scored for you to develop your inner consciousness and to let your individuality blossom forth.

CHAPTER – 2

ANUBHAVA

MAHATAMA GANDHI
BIRTH : October 02, 1869
DEATH: January 30, 1948
"To believe in something,
and not to live it, is
dishonest."

A verse by Shakeel Badayuni, quoted and translated by Dr. Karan Singh in an article.
Har cheez nahin hai markaz par,
Ek zarra idhar ek zarra udhar.
Nafrat se na dekho dushman ko,
Shaayad woh mohabbat kar baithe.
(Urdu, alphabet in English)
Things are not always in equilibrium,
A slight tilt this way a slight tilt that,
Look not with hatred upon the enemy,
He may end up loving you.

A normally living person may not have an enemy as such. However, one is likely to have known a person, who one may dislike intensely. This hatred may be caused by a slew of reasons. As per one's experience up to date one would have reached a final view point of hatred with the person. For sake of various personal and mindful benefits, the wise people advise the hatred to be dropped like a hot potato.

It is desirable indeed, to follow the advice for the sake of normalcy of one's blood pressure even though one may be in disagreement. This would call for a change of attitude. Pluralistically speaking, a change of attitudes would result in Transformation of Personality.

Following is a critical comment, finally resulting in a very delectable, sublime suggestion by J. Krishnamurti.

Is it really possible to change ourselves?

A change is possible only from the known to unknown, not from the known to known. There comes into being a hierarchical outlook of life—You know, I do not know so I worship you. Thus got created a system; go after a *guru*.

This change is a very exhilarating feeling. None other is comparable. This is a kind of self-revelation. A sudden beam of knowledge strikes the receiver. One feels as if dark corner of mind and intellect have simultaneously lit up. An essential requirement here is a perceptive mind.

Essential Pre-requisites for the Receptive mind.

The beliefs and principles we value have to be firmly preserved. This is to be achieved even at the cost of necessary sacrifices. Emphasis has been laid on three aspects of one's self in this context viz. (a) Intellectual (b) Emotional and (c) Physical. Ganapati Sachidananda Swamiji holds,

The facts of self and relative principles are :-

(a) Intellectual   Fearlessness
(b) Emotional   Non-attachment
(c) Physical   Non-Violence

The superior level of intellect is streaming through all human thought and action. This gift of nature distinguishes humans from animals. Hence, our level of perception, discretion, discrimination and discernment. This is 'Viveka', the lifeline of righteousness. Our capacity to be discreet would guide us to think why fear?

One can surely discriminate between the imaginary snake and a rope lying in shady darkness. The real can be discerned from the imagined shadow of fear. Life has gone on, after all fear only worsens the situation and reduces the capacity to face what is real.

'Viveka' (meaning depth and width of understanding) is gained from enlightenment. Acharya Mahaprajna states that the mind and instincts go hand in hand, through a state of enlightenment. Every action of such a person is rational even though mind remains involved in each action. Every activity of the body becomes a conscious activity. Even instinctive activities take place under the auspices of consciousness. This wakefulness is the consequence of a stage achieved in the transformation of personality. Thinking and doing become a unity.

With the further progress in the path of meditation ('sadhana'), self consciousness is the next stage of transformation. It brings about a dispassionate attitude of mind.

Once we get a glimpse of our native existence, we begin to command discernment which is a pre-condition of the regeneration of man. Discernment enables us to develop a neutral attitude of mind. It is the first result of the perception of our real existence. Neutrality is the next result.

The neutral man is neither inclined towards pleasing things nor disinclined towards unpleasing things because he commands mental equilibrium or a sense of equality. **Discernment** produces neutrality, neutrality produces indifference and indifference brings about a balanced mind.

The above sequence of steps guides one to an apex of moral living in this world, indicated by great religions recognized in the civilized society. A complete reconstitution of personality is the end product of 'sadhana' (practice to adopt self-consciousness and meditation). It implies a surrender of the empirical self or personality. This surrender leads to emergence of man's real and unqualified existence. The boundary of unqualified existence of the self begins where the boundary of the empirical self ends. This is the outcome of 'sadhana'. Whether this is achievable by the mortal human being as a worldly individual, is a different matter. A number of great men, some known others unknown have done it.

Keeping the focus on a worldly human being Sri Jaggi Vasudev said, the body is only a heap of food and the mind an accumulation of impressions. To amass all this there must be something within but this is not in our experience. So the process of turning inward is another dimension, it exists as a possibility. When one experiences oneself there is harmony.

Peace and joy are intrinsic to human nature. When a person pursues happiness he is in conflict with the existence because he will want to get rid of anything that stands in the way of his desired objective. Even if he does not have the stamina, he has the emotion. Thus human pursuit of happiness has caused enormous damage to this planet, on the other hand if he is joyful by nature he will act with clarity and intelligence; one who is in pursuit of happiness acts with a sense of desperation.

Once Adi Sankara said in 'Vivekchudamani', "For all beings, the mind alone is the cause of bondage and freedom". An agitated mind binds man to his passion for experience. While the same mind, freed from passions, is the instrument to become *'jiwan mukta'* (free from bondage of life's shackles), who performs his worldly duties by remaining in perfect harmony with his inner self and the universal self.

We feel elated on success and dejected on failure. We remain embroiled in miseries. The goal is a steady mind where the pairs of opposites do not bother us.

Calm your mind for more efficiency, says Swami Swaroopananda

"My lord, mind is like wind, it is very difficult to control?" is the epic question raised by warrior king Arjuna to Lord Krishna in Srimad Bhagavad Gita.

Suggestion to apply reigns to the five horses of the mind has emerged. Practice meditation in a quiet clean spot in the house at a silent time of the day. Sit with least discomfort, back, neck and head in a straight line, hands gently on your lap (possibly one palm over the other). Body though in comfort, not to move. Tell the partial feeling of discomfort to relax. Mentally massage the part appearing as restless against the rest of the body which is steady. As one learns to relax the body, the mind also relaxes.

Thoughts will come to mind. Do not panic. Shift the attention of the mind to the steady body. Become a spectator of a beautiful motionless statue. When the body is motionless, it also slowly quiets down.

Practice 10-15 minutes, 3 times a day. Pressure of work ought not to be a deterrent. Each day be ready for a new lesson, new experience in quietude to experience greater peace and joy. Oh yes, let the prescription dosage be adapted to personal suitability.

CHAPTER – 3

MIND

GAUTAMA BUDDHA
Born: c. 563 B.C.E.
Died: c. 483 B.C.E.
Do not dwell in the past, do not dream of the future, concentrate the mind on the present moment.

Before the birth, in so far as heredity is a part of conception, the concepts of knowledge are transported by the vehicle of genes from one generation to the next. Only thereafter the bundles of experience get gifted by the environment, the circumstance, the universe. This individual's world has an interlink with the self, THE MIND. What is this MIND? Let us see.

Mind, the all-powerful storehouse

Swami Vivekananda metaphorically described the mind as a monkey that has drunk wine, is bitten by a scorpion and has a demon inside him. Human mind is like a restless monkey, drunk with the wine of desire, bitten by jealousy and possessed by the demon of pride. To control mind, one must go deep down into the subconscious mind and subdue all thoughts. Only a controlled mind can successfully meditate on the Supreme Self.

Restless nature, drunk of desire. Bitten by Scorpion of Jealousy, possessed by demon of pride.

Meditating means forgetting everything, to eat, drink, sleep, and any other physical and mental comforts, when immersed in a subject of choice.

Writers, poets, musicians often absorb themselves in their work and come up with remarkable compositions that already existed within them. A spiritualist's choice is meditating upon the self.

To reach the goal of meditation one must adopt the following eight rules: 1. *Yama*—not injuring any one by thought, word or deed, non-covetousness in thought, word or deed, perfect chastity by word, thought or deed, truthfulness in thought, word or deed, non-receiving of unethical gifts. 2. *Niyama*—bodily purity. 3. *Asana*—straight posture of spine. 4. *Pranayama*—controlling breath. 5. *Pratayahara*—turning the mind inward. 6. *Dhaarana*—firmness to hold on to moral concepts. 7. *Dhyana*—meditation, concentration on one subject. 8. *Samadhi*—illumination.

A Yogi is superior to a man of action. So, *'Tasmat yogi bhava Arjuna'*, (May you be a yogi, Arjuna) (Geeta, 6.46). To get power over nature one must meditate, a fact, which Einstein too admitted. Meditation is the direct method to uplift the mind to a height of endless joy.

Mind is not a dustbin

People tend to park their ill feelings, jealousy, anxiety, hatred and what not in their minds.

Don't let the mind retain just your bad and depressing thoughts. Look and act positive, your face will glow.

Yes, the mind is a 'Temple of God'. How sacred it should be is not beyond one's imagination. So rejoice. Let joyful thoughts gladden the mind. Present is the season for rejoicing and filling the mind with glad tiding.

Depart goodness, enter evil

Where does evil come from? Is it an unseen malevolent force God didn't reckon with, or is it entirely man made?

As parts of God, we can choose evil over good. We can stand in light or shadow.

It was a tenet of the Bolsheviks that their citizens believed first and foremost in Lenin and the state. God was purged. Millions of Stalin's subjects died. But after 70 years, with the appearance of glasnost and perestroika, church, synagogue, mosque and temple attendance doubled. This indicates an innateness of God consciousness.

How we respond to everyday life determines whether good or evil triumphs. Sharp vision conquers even ideology gone wrong. The trick is to follow God's road map with all our talents and to stay awake, taking every opportunity to advance along the path of life. This, an advice from Mukunda Goswami.

Say Goodbye to Negativity

Yogic wisdom of Swami Gokulananda of Rama Krishna Mission as expanded by Bhawana Gera is easily intelligible as follows.

Negative emotions

Greed, hatred, jealousy, dishonesty and other negative emotions have penetrated deep into our psyche as we forget the importance of religion in our lives. We are slowly becoming slaves to these feelings that are eating away the very foundations on which this society is based and can be sustained.

Overcoming Negativity

To subjugate all negative emotions, you need to subject yourself to spiritual discipline. You must practice fourfold sadhanas—the synthesis of four yogas—Karma Yoga, Jnana Yoga, Bhakti Yoga and Raja Yoga.

Karma Yoga

Karma Yoga teaches us to act with the spirit of detachment. You need to work vigorously but also be able to surrender the fruit of our actions to the Lord. Make it your daily practice to do whatever has been assigned to you without worrying about its consequences, be it working as a teacher or sweeping the floor. Never think that you are the director, you play the role faithfully and actions will go on automatically.

Jnana Yoga

Jnana yoga teaches to us to discriminate. You have to discriminate every day between the good and the bad, the right and the wrong.

Bhakti Yoga

Bhakti yoga or the path of devotion teaches all of us to love others irrespective of their colour, caste, creed and wealth. Anyone who tries to find God in temples will always fail to do so if he is not engaged in the service of the poor, the afflicted and the downtrodden. This 'Para Bhakti', is the highest form of Bhakti. A devotee engaged in the latter sees the Lord and Lord alone everywhere and experiences His power manifested in different ways.

Raja Yoga

Raja Yoga or the science of meditation exhorts us to meditate daily. You should earmark a few minutes for holding communion with your inner self or God. It is spending some time quietly in self-analysis, introspection and other such inward directed activities.

The daily practice of these four forms of yoga helps you face and conquer circumstances in the present and future. Without it, you cannot have either the present or the future.

Control fickleness of the mind

Acharya Mahaprajna advises, those who are restless cannot deny the desires of the mind, which will go on increasing. And they will continue fulfilling them one after the other incessantly.

Prekshadhyana is the practice of discretion when engaging in a thought process or action. A person who knows how to live in the present moment, is facilitated by five factors, namely: awareness, keen interest, profound meditation, effort and indifference to desires.

The five factors for living in the present moment will lead to a new style of effective living.

Our philosophy dictates our actions

Swami Nikhilananda states, each one of us has a philosophy about Ishwara or God. God as being just and compassionate, taking care of us and being loving. Others may take God to be an autocratic entity with no concern about the world.

We have an image about ourselves, God, the world and our relationship.

We have a vision regarding ethics, working, religion, rituals, in fact everything of consequence and even our most insignificant actions are rooted in this. Different people would respond differently to being pushed in the bus.

Arjuna came to the battlefield to fight the Kauravas with revenge and anger in his heart.

Through the shlokas of the Bhagawad Geeta the Lord changed Arjuna's philosophy, made him take stock of the situation and helped him to respond or fight without anger.

Face adversity bravely to attain divinity

A.C. Jose is hard to digest when he states that all those who long for divine excellence know that the misfortunes which the Lord apportions us in His infinite love and grace are the surest and quickest route to make us advance. And the harder the misfortunes the more they perceive the greatness of the Divine Love.

God is a must and evil is a mask; both are apparently eidola. We must resolutely remove the mask and see only the face of God behind it.

For that which is within us, is the Divine presence, and that which is in others, is the same Divine presence.

And the whole world becomes a holy place and all cause of fear or grief or hatred disappears.

Being content: It's all in mind

If a person lives a good life, it may be assumed that he'll achieve a corresponding measure of contentment. To think of contentment as itself a virtue, however is like "putting the cart before the horse".

Contentment is, in fact, a state of mind. It must be actively practised, not anticipated for some future time.

Contentment must be a deliberately assumed mental attitude; it doesn't depend on outward circumstances, and in fact the more people anticipate in the future, the less ability they have to enjoy it fully in the present.

Above an excellent piece of advice by Swami Kriyananda.

Method to control the mind is suggested by Acharya Mahaprajna

Breath is the means of controlling the fickleness of the mind. By controlling breath, you can control the mind. That is why we have taken breath as the basis of our exercises.

Breath travels inside the body as well as outside it. It is like a lamp which illuminates the somatic as well as extra-spasmodic atmosphere in the midst of which man lives. In other words let us become introverts. That is the essence of spirituality. The mind has got to be yoked to breath. This is the first step of energizing ourselves.

Philosophers have discussed the nature of 'sat' (that which exists) and 'asat' (that which does not exist). 'Asat' is that which has no activity. 'Sat' is that which has activity.

That which has energy as well as consciousness is called a living being. Atoms have energy but they do not posses consciousness. The soul has both energy and consciousness.

Let thoughts come and go

There is no sense in repeating sacred formulae. Repetition of formulae can be fruitful only if the repetition is accompanied by 'bhavana' or suggestions.

One may go on repeating the formula, "This world and the body are transient" for years and years together, but it will produce no effect unless it is accompanied by the mood associated with the transience of the world or unless it acts as a suggestion. This feeling or mood has to be imbibed by one who repeats the formula.

Let the thought processes, whatever their content, come and go. But instead of indulging in them be a mere spectator. The effect of our past actions and experiences accumulated in the subconscious mind must one day or the other find their expression. Let them express themselves.

Leadership is choice by mind

Whatever we are today is the direct consequence of choices we made and decisions we took. Our 'karma' cannot be shared. It is non-transferable. Leadership, and indeed life itself, is primarily about making decisions.

Leadership, at its core, is not just about taking decisions but also about taking absolute and full responsibility for them and their consequence irrespective of the way things work out.

General Patton's view that "a good plan today is better than a perfect plan tomorrow" holds as true in today's corporate and philosophical battlegrounds as it did on the killing fields of World War II.

There will always be those who will attribute motives to all decisions, much in the way the Opposition does in today's political arena, irrespective of which party plays the role at any given point.

The individual who aspires to grow as a leader must therefore learn to stop looking for universal approbation when he makes a decision and pays heed to Swami Vivekananda : "This I have seen is life—he who is over-cautious about himself, falls into dangers at every step; he who is afraid of losing honour and respect, gets only disgrace; he who is always afraid of loss, always loses".

Krishna advised Arjuna: "Thus has wisdom more secret than all secrets, been declared to thee by Me. Having reflected on it fully do as thou choosest". *(Gita, 18.63)*. The final decision—and responsibility for its consequences—was left to Arjuna.

Hindrance by the senses

Ashutosh Ji Maharaj emphasizes the role of senses on mind's susceptibility. The Human mind has a tendency to get attracted to the lure of the senses. Our senses make us run outward as we have not learnt to train and tame the mind.

The spirit of renunciation does not come easily. It has to be earned with persistence; determination and discrimination. The task is all the more difficult as the advertising world and television channels seem, knowingly or unknowingly, to be involved in a conspiracy to give fillip to the senses.

Gautama Buddha gave us a rule of thumb to deal with and win over the senses. He called it the middle path. It is not consumption but unrestrained indulgence which is bad for health and happiness.

Free the mind off, passions

Once Aadi Sankara said in Vivekchudamni: "For all beings, the mind alone is the cause of bondage and freedom." An agitated mind binds man to his passion for experiences. While the same mind, freed from passions, is the instrument to become a jivan mukta who performs his worldly duties by remaining in perfect harmony with his inner self and the Universal Self.

As is the mind, so is the man. Happiness is attained by those who fully comprehend the quirks of the mind. Then the process of subduing the mind starts. As the world is constantly changing, so the uncontrolled mind keeps bombarding with positive/negative impulses. We feel elated on success and dejected on failure. We remain embroiled in miseries. The goal is a steady mind where the pairs of opposites do not bother us.

Be at home with yourself

J. Krishnamurti, the enlightened mystic, once said: "We gossip about others because we are not sufficiently interested in the process of our own thinking and our own action."

Life is really very precious and if we realize this, we will have no time for petty things. Instead we will utilize our time in raising our own consciousness.

The Russian mystic Gurdjieff used to say: "We live in such a sleepy state of consciousness that if we really count the minutes we spend when we are really aware, fully conscious, it will be not more than five minutes in all the 60 years.

Out of this, the 20 years are spent in sleeping. While the rest of the 40 years are spent in day-dreaming, fulfilling our ambitions and desires, and chasing mirages. And in the end we find really nothing in our hands.

Meditation takes us beyond these ripples, and there we are at home.

The key to contentment lies in being grateful to God for what you have got. Mind runs after things, more often than not, contrary to destiny. For those who believe that destiny can be molded by oneself. I have to say that even the confidence in 'Purushartha' (efforts by self) is a part of destiny. A fraction of faith in destiny will result in a bounty of contentment.

CHAPTER – 4

RESOLVE!

Action follows when you resolve

ALEXANDER
BIRTH DATE: c. 356 BCE
DEATH DATE: c. 323 BCE
There is nothing impossible to him who will try.

Life is being and becoming. We exist; that is being. We desire; that is becoming. Each one of us wants to be something other than what we are.

It is our nature to be preoccupied with results and it is this that gives rise to problems.

We tend to have a superficial view of things; we should go deeper to know the truth. We need to distinguish between disposition and essential nature. Mere preoccupation misleads, producing illusion. Do away with anger, evil, ignorance, indiscipline, aggression and acquisitiveness. Probe deeper. Truth will reveal itself. Don't be concerned only with removing ills; try to understand the phenomenon.

Psychologists say that a particular nature gives rise to certain tendencies with its attendant consequences. "To achieve non-violence or continence or non-acquisitiveness through an effort of will?" They say it can be done. We exercise our will. We determine not to indulge in violence, not to tell lies, not to steal, not to be acquisitive.

To resolve to do or not to do something is not enough. If one could ensure non-violence through mere exertion of one's will it would be wonderful. Each man would take a vow not to remain poor, and there would be no more poverty.

Spiritual thinkers advocate the disciplining of mind, body and tongue. With discipline comes fulfillment and non-violence. If the mind is still, non-violence comes into being. If the mind is pure and still, continence follows; and non-greed. The thoughts, as expressed by Acharya Mahaprajna.

The driving force is purity

Water purity, air purity, food purity—all are in vogue and considered vital. But what about consciousness purity? It makes sense that clarity of mind is also important. That there is power in purity should be examined. T.S. Eliot wrote, "Power is present, holiness is hereafter". But the poet missed something. How about "Purity is the force", a Chinese epigram that stimulates another dimension in thought?

Power often refers to something that generates energy. Force, however tiny and insignificant, has grown and influenced people of earth. The history of great ideas and people of distinction began with a microscopic, germ-like, single celled substance that grew into a human embryo.

And it was anthropologist Margaret Mead who said, "Never doubt the ability of a small group of committed people to change the world."

If we actively promote purity of mind and body, we will have embarked on the road to well being and created a significant incentive to foster goodness in the world, so says Mukunda Goswami.

Compromising on ideals not needed

Getting along with people doesn't mean agreeing with everybody, and it doesn't mean you should sacrifice your ideals for their sake. That is not the getting along. But you can maintain your ideals without being offensive. So above everything else, please God and live up to your own ideals; never harbor an ulterior motive. If you can live loving God, meaning no harm to anyone, and still the world wants to hurt you, that is alright.

During my earliest years in the United States, I was once invited as a guest of honour to a large party.

Late into the evening, they asked me to speak, so I gave them a talk that I think they never forget. I did not speak in anger, but in truth. "Is this your natural way of life? Are you really happy embalming yourself in drink? This is not fun, getting dead drunk and talking in an evil way. What is this?

Behave in a truthful way that isn't hurtful to others. If you cannot get along with others because of your ideals, then it's best to get away from these naysayers. This, a sermon by Sri Sri Paramhans Yogananda.

What keeps you going is important

A.K. Bhargava expresses what keeps us going is the one without which one finds no purpose in life. Wealth keeps most of us going in life. But is that the ultimate thing?

The workaholic thinks that he will be able to work forever. The family-oriented person thinks that his children will be with him. All physical things, emotions and knowledge do not last and keep changing. If we cultivate something in life, which is our focal point and which, is unchanging and nonperishable, we will find meaning. That everlasting thing is nothing else but the trust, faith and love for God. Make 'Adhyaatma' the focal point which means that all roads of knowledge and experience lead to one's soul.

Be Free of mental cob-webs

The nature of the mind is always to accumulate. When it is gross, it wants to accumulate things. When it becomes a little more evolved, it wants to accumulate knowledge. When emotion becomes dominant, it wants to accumulate people around oneself. But the basic nature is, it wants to accumulate.

When a person starts thinking or believing that he is on a spiritual path, then the mind starts to accumulate so-called spiritual wisdom. Until one goes beyond the need to accumulate, knowledge or wisdom—it means there is an insufficiency.

With awareness and constant *sadhana*, (meditation), slowly, the vessel becomes totally empty.

But if you become empty enough for Grace to descend, then the ultimate nature is within reach. It is here to be experienced and realized.

It is going beyond all dimensions of existence, into the exalted state. It is not tomorrow, not another lifetime. It becomes a living reality.

The web of bondage is constantly being woven only by the way we think and feel. Whatever we are calling as awareness is just to start creating a distance between all that you think, feel and yourself. Sadhana(Practice of Meditation) is an opportunity to raise your energies so that you can tide over these limitations with which you have entangled your thoughts and emotions.

The aforesaid thoughts emanate from Sadh Guru Jaggi Vasedev.

Health is Wealth

Individuals become vulnerable to disease and stress at an early age because of the pressure they inflict on themselves in an effort to fulfill their high ambitions or misplaced priorities.

It is fundamentally necessary for our holistic development to re-appraise our aspirations and pursue only firm priorities. Such priorities include firm time allocations for exercise, leisure, family, spiritual inquiry, reading etc. In synergizing these activities along with our work objectivism we will definitely be more focused and productive.

The pressure of living in contemporary urban environment, linked to our various work commitments sometimes leads to a lifestyle, wherein we flow along at a very frantic pace. Even housewives in large metros have very busy routines and very little time to nurture themselves. In adopting several holistic techniques to keep our minds, bodies and soul in balance, we should include the necessity of short holidays.

We must always take the initiative of driving out to the countryside for a few days of peace, quiet and meditation. Just breathing air, which has high oxygen content, every few months, does wonders for our holistic health. So says, Vikram Raina.

Within our-self, a wonder kid

The voice of conscience never tells a lie. To listen to our inner voice, we needn't be supernaturally evolved. We just need to be truly honest.

Maharishi Ramanna too emphasized engaging in self-inquiry to reclaim true vision. In course of time, the veils of illusion and ignorance are lifted and the sense of our mission is regained.

The Bible says God made man in His own image. From this, it can be inferred that man being essentially divine, should possess infinite capacity to change himself and his surroundings. This calls for realizing our essential divinity.

The burgeoning informational deluge of today should not satisfy us. All knowledge is within. We are a microcosm with all the macrocosm within us. Each of us is a wonder kid. Strive to unearth and re-discover the wisdom wrapped in innate divinity. Mission on Earth will be fulfilled only on realizing it. These words by S.K. Vasudeva.

The basis of top achievement is faith

Faith looks beyond all boundaries, transcends limitations, penetrates all obstructions and sees the goal. Faith is the basis of every act.

You should believe in the inner motivator, the *atman* within, the voice of God.

Once you start charging your mind with dynamic and positive thoughts, the subconscious mind starts generating the much-needed 'power'. Despair and disappointments vanish like ghosts in daylight.

These new and fascinating heights can be scaled if you develop faith in that supreme power dwelling in you. It was this faith, the eternal elixir, which enabled Gandhi to fight against a mighty empire. It was this faith that enabled Lincoln to abolish slavery. These thoughts by Suman Dayal Prasad.

The evil in disguise

We can easily tell, by instinct, that certain acts, such as murder, rape, theft, robbery, extortion, child abuse and so forth belong to the dark side of creation.

Unfortunately, few are able to recognize and fight "clean" faced evil. For, it comes subtly and slowly, affecting the masses like an epidemic. It does not demand active decision, but passive indifference or thoughtlessness towards a sugar-coated vice.

In her book *The life of the mind*, Hannah Arendt expresses shock over the thoughtlessness of a Nazi official revealed during his trial for numerous evil acts meted out on hapless Jews in a concentration camp in his acquiescent obedience to his seniors.

She says, "I was struck by a manifest shallowness in the doer that made it impossible to trace the incontestable evil of his deeds to any deeper level of roots or motives.

The deeds were monstrous, but the doer—at least the very effective one now on trial was quite ordinary, commonplace, and neither demonic nor monstrous. It was not stupidity but thoughtlessness."

C.S. Lewis, a well-known thinker has also noted, "The greatest evil is not done in those sordid 'dens of crime'. It is conceived and moved, seconded, carried, and minuted in clean, carpeted, warmed, and well lighted offices, by quiet men with white collars.

Let us guard ourselves against evil in disguise by consciously questioning the roots and motives of the practices in the world.

'Jiva' and the transcendental

Despite our ignorance, the soul is always inclined towards its source. The *Jiva* remains restless till it takes refuge in the Lord. In this return journey, the mind is the biggest obstacle. It acts like a screen on our consciousness.

We are being led astray every moment. Due to the overbearing influence that the mind exerts, we are contented living in a fool's paradise.

Turning inward is the answer but for this inner voyage, the divine eye is needed. A true saint does just this, he actively helps you in the process and does not fill your head with flowery sermons and speeches.

It is a transcendental experience of the divine, which is both the insignia and the litmus test to judge the worthiness of the preceptor. As expressed by Ashutosh ji Maharaj.

Change the world with an 'ideal'

As an individual each one of us has duties towards oneself, family members, and society and as a global citizen, towards one's chosen profession. But in our blind pursuit for happiness in the world, we ignore and refuse these sacred duties. In our selfishness, our children get neglected; the youth are misguided with no proper guidance or a clear goal in life. And all this leads to confusion, demoralization and corruption everywhere within our hearts and in the world around.

Neither can we bring about the development of individuals nor of the country until people cultivate the right attitude. People must have an ideal that will change the whole attitude of the people. We must have an ideal that will help in bringing citizens together and work selflessly for the material and spiritual welfare of all or Loka Samagraha.

The unseen thread that can hold the people together as an integrated nation is this inspiring ideal, which will have a strong foundation in a rich and ancient culture, and its philosophical vision of the Shastras (Scriptures).

Health of mind and body make-up wealth

The world adores strength, not weakness. If on the cricket grounds the batsman strikes a number of sixers in succession, young men applaud in great excitement, dance in delight and lift him up. Isn't it an adoration of strength, energy and drive? It is said, "If we become weak, even our friends turn into foes."

Wisdom lies in increasing our strength in everyway. We should develop not only our body and mind, our intellectual and ethical powers but also strength of our soul.

Swami Vivekananda said 'Strength is life, weakness is death. Strength is felicity, life eternal, immortal, weakness is constant strain and misery, weakness is death".

The weak man not only gets destroyed. He instills in others the tendency towards exploitation and perpetration of violence.

In each individual there exists a divine force, which is beyond death and decay. It is present in everybody. The forces needed to sustain life: guidance, strength, support, inspiration, etc. are within us. How is it then that in spite of holding within us such unlimited powers, we behave like slaves? So says Swami Jagadatmananda.

The task on hand needs focus

It is best then to focus on the job in hand. Whether it is studies, running a business, pursuing a profession to achieve the higher goal, complete dedication is needed. To focus, one does not try to achieve too many things at the same time. The quality of the result is best brought out by single minded devotion.

There are certain basics needed for practicing Karam Yoga. In Swami Shivender's words, for any 'karma' (duty), the essentials are your inherent nature (Swadharma), higher cause and an attitude of gratitude for the result. Once your *karma* has these elements, it is bound to be *satvik* (pure) and by doing such karmas (tasks) you practice *karma yoga.*

"Do not lose sight of what you have to achieve and all will come to you. Sunset may take long to come, but a new sun will rise only after the sun sets, puts the advice in words, A.K. Bhargava.

The will to change

When a bad habit is fixed in your mind and you want to change it, you will have to use your strong will to pulverize that habit and absorb it into fresh, pliable good actions that can be remoulded to the desired image. Strong will means strong conviction. The minute you say to yourself, "I am not bound by this habit," this means the habit will be gone.

Discrimination is your keen eyesight and will is your power of locomotion. Without will, you may know what is right through discrimination and yet not act on it. It is acting on knowledge that gets you to your goal. Both discrimination and will are necessary. Will power is easy to develop. Try first for small accomplishments. Gradually you will get rid of tendencies you thought you could not overcome. Watch your consciousness. Develop the habit of self-examination, of watching and analyzing the thoughts and behaviors.

The thoughts are attributed to Sri Paramhans Yogananda.

Sex : The tempest

A news item dated August 20, 2004 from New Delhi, reported as follows.

Youngsters, swinging under the influence of Ecstasy, heroin, charas and *'ganja'* are a common sight at rave parties and nightclubs. According to the narcotics branch, the number of drug addicts in Delhi has risen steeply. The students form a major chunk.

But what is really alarming is the easy availability of drugs, popular as *'Maal'* or *'Pudia'*, in and around the North Campus area.

In 2001, a law was passed that allows persons smuggling less than 250 gram of heroin to get bail. The peddlers have been taking advantage of this flaw.

And now, Sat.porn

The above news was preceded by a news report dated August 14th, 2004.

Direct-to-home (DTH) is now proving to be a boon to pornography lovers and it's something the government didn't anticipate. Viewers have lately been accessing 24 hour adult programming from around the world on their TV, through a combination of a satellite dish, decoder, and dedicated smart cards. And there's nothing the law can do about it.

Industry sources say X-rated smart cards, on sale for Rs. 5,000 to 7,000 are being smuggled in bulk into India from Southeast Asian countries through Mumbai. These cards allow anyone using a DTH decoder to access signals of adult channels directly from the transmitting satellite.

The most popular porn bouquet comes from the *Blue Kiss* network, with one free-to-air and two pay channels. It's available on Asia Sat, which is easily accessible in India. These cards also allow viewers to download a lot of Russian porn channels. Some cards are also arriving from England, where a DTH network boasts of a dozen porn channels.

Top I&B ministry officials confess they never foresaw this problem when DTH guidelines were framed.

They feel satellite porn might force the government to revisit those guidelines.

"There is no need for people now to buy cheap pirated cassettes or CDs of porn films." They say. "All they need to do is insert the card in the decoder."

Jawahar Goyal, chief of the Zee Group's Dish TV, admitted porn was available but said it was for the government to formulate a policy to check "misuse" of DTH technology. "The industry is willing to provide all help to the government," he said.

Alternate sexuality is capital catchment

On the same date the city edition of a leading News Paper carried the following titles and details.

'Coming out' is easier, but it's usually about sex

As the police try and figure out whether the double murder in Anand Lok is a 'crime of passion' involving two homosexuals, the issue of alternate sexuality—and its spiralling growth—is back in focus yet again.

Furtive glances and questions stammered out at the risk of getting beaten up are a thing of the past, at least in the metros. Technology, more than anything else, has empowered the homosexual. While the increasing occurrence of gay and lesbian characters both on TV and movies has helped make attitudes more liberal, the internet and mobile phones have introduced new ways of establishing contact.

The Nigah Media Collective tries to organize meetings on the second and last Friday of every month.

According to an ad on their website, the last meeting took place in Defence Colony on August 13.

It had "readings from *The Vagina Monologues,* original poetry, spoken word performances and live music". Formed in 2003, Nigah tries to use different forms of media to initiate discussions around issues of gender and sexuality. Organizations like Nigah are leading the way as far as approaching a "gay culture" goes.

But the need for sex continues to drive most people to eplore a variety of avenues. During a trip to Mumbai around a year ago, a couple of gay friends decided to "pick up" guys. While one chatted up a middle-aged Russian sailor in a bar, the other paid a boy along Marine Drive. Both say the gay scene in Mumbai is thriving: they talked about pubs and discos setting aside nights for "special gay evenings" and pointed out young men—some in drag—soliciting.

The gay scene in Delhi may not be as in your-face as Mumbai but its there, Pubs and discos have been known to set aside nights and parties are also organized on a regular basis. To attend, you have to be in the know. Invites are usually sent out using e-mail.

Double murder outs Delhi's gay culture

In a double homicide that threatens to "out" Delhi's up market homosexual culture, two men, one naked and the other semi-nude, were found murdered in South Delhi's posh Anand Lok on Saturday morning.

One of the victims was Pushkin Chandra, a 38-years old project development officer with USAID who lived in the outhouse and whose father is a retired IAS officer. He was found in his bathroom, naked, his hands and legs tied and his throat slit. He'd been stabbed in his neck and abdomen.

The other was Vishal, in his 20s, found on the bed in his Bermudas and a vest, his hands and legs tied and throat slit.

That's not all. The police found hundreds of photos of naked men in homosexual acts as well as porn VCDs in the bedroom. Some photos show men in women's clothing, and some even have names written on them. It isn't clear if the killers were looking for specific pictures, but the Polaroid camera used is missing. Also gone is Pushkin's Opel Corsa.

Adding to the mystery is the fact the police found no fingerprints or footprints at the scene of the crime. They did find two knives, one of which was broken—possibly the murder weapon. They also found several empty liquor bottles, leading them to suspect that recreational drugs may have played a role.

Stay calm in the midst of Sex tempest

Mayhem, Chaos, turmoil, insanity, upheaval, pandemonium. Whatever you choose to call the way we live now, it's a fast, swirling mindless merry go round, a roller coaster ride in the theme-less park of planet earth. Dizzy, confused and sometimes nauseating, the show goes on. A stanza in the Gita rings out above all others in this regard.

The verse (2.70) reads, "a person who is not disturbed by the incessant flow of desires that enter like rivers into the ocean, which is ever being filled but is always still—can alone achieve peace, and not the man who strives to satisfy such desires."

42

The passage intimates we can live and think quietly, even when chaos and madness frolic all around us. We're assailed non-stop, especially in today's fast-paced world, by literally thousands of propositions that offer happiness. But the person of true peacefulness, like the ocean, is unaffected by constant enticements. The advice is by Mukunda Goswami.

Alter-ego converts to sublime desire

I want peace, every human being, at every stage of life, thinks it and says and demands it. Seekers ask sages and saints the way. And the latter give a trite prescription.

Remove the want and destroy the I and what have you? Peace, Peace, Peace. Extinguish Desire and kill the Identity and you will have 'shanti', 'shanti', 'shanti'. The question here is not whether we can banish ego and desire. Should humans abandon ego and suppress desire at all? Or, the real objective should be to raise our ego and desire to a higher plane? Most of us believe that history's saints and sages like Christ, Mohammad, Guru Nanak, Ramakrishna Paramahamsa, Vivekananda and those of our own times like Sai Baba, Mahatma Gandhi, Kanchi Paramacharya, Maharishi Ramanna and Mother Teresa to be egoless and desireless. The common perception of saintliness and spirituality is that the object of worship must be a person dead from the neck down, devoid of fleshy wants and earthly desires and sweetly smiling all the time.

We want them to rid us of our baser instincts, drives and relationships.

We seek advice and guidance, not on how to live life with zest, hope and enthusiasm but how best to repress our instincts, deny our feelings and utilize our energies. All things that frighten us, torment us and confuse us, we think that the sage is untouched by them. It is this void, this absence, which is perceived as egolessness.

The human ego is not an obstruction to the human spirit but a dynamic and radiant manifestation of spirit. It is not necessary to get rid of one's ego but simply to live with it and endow it a certain external thrust towards the cosmic reality. We need our ego to move from the small self to the big self. These thoughts have been put into words by V.N. Narayanan.

No doormat, quiet and firm

Sri Sri Paramahansa Yogananda says, in your effort to get along with others 'do not be a doormat' or everyone will want to run your life for you.

When you find resistance to your ideals the best way is to just remain quiet but firm. Say nothing. Do not get angry. Refuse to quarrel. Eventually those persons will understand that you do not mean to anger them. When someone has made up his mind to win a point let him have the victory, it is a hollow victory. Don't argue. Great men seldom argue; they smile and say, "I don't think so", but they do not fight.

Smart work begets better performance

In his book author Pramod Batra has related the well known story of the hare and tortoise race, various ways and environs where the two challenges again to win and lose alternately and they eventually reach the goal together best as a team.

They ultimately use the core competencies of tortoise to swim and the hare to run fast carrying each other in turns.

Six morals of the story as enumerated by Pramod Batra need to be appreciated as a way of *'Karm-Yoga'* in different environments.

1. Slow and steady wins the race.
2. Fast and consistent will always beat the slow and steady. It's good to be slow and steady but it's better to be fast and consistent.
3. First, identify your core competency and then change the playing field to suit your core competency. Working on the basis of your strengths will not only get you noticed, but will also create opportunities for growth and advancement.
4. It is good to be individually motivated and to have strong core competencies: but unless you're able to work in a team and harness each other's core competencies, you'll always perform below par.
5. In life, when faced with a failure, sometimes it is appropriate to work harder and to put in more effort by working smarter. Sometimes, you just have to change strategy and try something different. And sometimes it is appropriate to do both.
6. When we stop competing against a rival and, instead, start competing against the situation, we perform far better

See what suits you out of these for better resolve and better performance.

CHAPTER – 5

EGO

ADOLF HITLER
BIRTH : April 20, 1889
DEATH: April 30, 1945

How fortunate for governments that the people they administer don't think.

Inflated beyond life-size capital I, that is Ego. Of utmost importance, in the forefront of all thoughts, recipient of all purposes, that is Ego. In the race to be more than equal amongst peers, better one if not the best amongst neighbors, there running at break-neck speed, that is Ego.

Personality given by one's family, developed within social environment is home to one's ego. It is not perceptible physically, realizable mentally, not observed critically with an objective view-point, but it governs one's thinking and course of actions. Everyone in calm moments feels that Ego is not desirable substantially but funny it is that it remains un-avoidable.

Then conversely why should one not think that it is desirable for progress and achievement. Without self confidence having traversed certain steps, how would one rise higher. The basic steps already taken, childhood onwards, appear to have helped the formation of Ego.

Naturally then Ego can be harmful and it can be useful, sort of two sides to a coin. Useful it would be but with a constructive approach plus the Ego based realistic confidence, avoiding any misconceived inflation thereof.

Ego breeds misconceived notions in life related to one's physique, knowledge, wealth, success and happiness. Arrogance is the prime diagnosis as a result of the aforesaid, for the diseased person that is an egotist.

To move some constructive steps ahead against this complex maize of the mental state of ego, let us discern this Ego vis-à-vis human being's personality.

Are we prisoners of our Ego

All human beings struggle constantly for happiness and in the process get entangled in some kind of crisis. We keep struggling for freedom and still get caught in some form of bondage. We strive for fame, but humiliation lies in wait to pounce on us. Right from birth till death, we are swept through the current of life by the conflicting waves of laughter and tears, hope and disappointment, love and hatred, victory and defeat.

Hence human beings are constantly in a state of restlessness. They seek happiness in wife and children, in wealth and worldly possessions. It is this desire that drives us to engage in acts that lead us to good or evil. But we are not guided by complete knowledge. It is only when we attain complete knowledge that we become free from bondage, attain perfection and experience perfect bliss.

But there is another struggle that's a constant in our lives. It's the struggle to maintain our ego.

As Bertrand Russell remarks in *The Conquest of Happiness:* "What people mean by the struggle for life is really the struggle for success. What people fear when they engage in the struggle is not that they will fail to get their breakfast next morning, but that they will fail to outshine their neighbors."

These views expressed by Swami Jagadatmananda.

Are we the undisputed kings of all we survey? If no, who are we?

The nature of man as depicted in the Indian scriptural literature and tradition is radically different from that of the west. The Judeo-Christian tradition tells us that the life of man is the result of the original sin and fall. Man is a sinner, and has to continually look for redemption with the help of an outside agency.

The Indian scriptures, on the other hand, describe man as *amritasya putrah* (children of immortal bliss). According to *Shrimad Bhagavatam* (XI, IX 28) "The divine one . . . projected the human form endowed with the capacity to realize Brahman—the universal divine self of all—and became extremely pleased". The *Aitreya Aranyaka* (II.13) declares that man is the abode of Brahman: *ayam purusha brahma-lokah.*

The faculty of memory in man coupled with the underlying unity of his experiences has led the Indian thinkers to conclude that there is an eternal, changeless and stable central entity in the core of man. Adi Shankaracharya states,

> "In his this entity, the core of a human being, knows everything that happens in the waking *(jagrata)*, dream *(swapana)* and deep sleep *(shsupti)* states. It knows the presence or absence of the mind and its functions. It is the basis of the egoism *(ahmkara)*."

Quotes from scriptures in this para are credited to Ashok Vora. However, it has to be stated in variance, that while *atman* is the all knowing core of a human being and the basis of egoism. 'Atman' is free of ego as also it is capable of shedding one's ego whenever willed as also adopt the ego when useful as a tool.

This core of man is *atman. Chandogya Upanishad* (Vii 25.2) proclaims that this *atman* is at the root of this manifested universe *(Idam sarvani yad ayam atman). Brihadaranyaka Upanishad* (II 5.19) categorically asserts that "this *atman* is Brahman". The essence of man, therefore, is nothing else but Brahman or *purusha. Mundaka Upanishad* (II.1.10) and (II.2.11) declares that *purusha* alone is all the universe". The manifested universe with all its apparent diversities is "only Brahman, the immortal—*Brahmaivedam amritan*".

The essential nature of *atman* is pure being, pure consciousness and bliss—*sat, cit ananda.* Like *atman*, Man too is not finite. He has to learn to see himself not as a truncated limited thing consisting merely of mind and body, which are nothing but instruments of his action in the spatio-temporal world, but as *atman*. Man alone has the capacity to realize the truth that his true nature is not that of a sinner but *nitya-shuddha-buddha-mukta svabhava parmatman*—the eternal, pure, awakened and free self.

He does not have to seek refuge in any person but search within himself. All that the gurus do is that they through their teachings create an atmosphere of alertness and constant seeking. One of the upper-most gurus to be mentioned in this context is Ramana Maharshi who layed persistent stress on the effort to query "who am I", who thinks up the thought, who is the core behind the mind.

Quotations from scriptures are by Ashok Vohra.

We suffer from Pride—a sign of immaturity

Pride goeth before destruction and a haughty spirit before a fall. Bible (Proverbs)

Pride sullies the noblest character—Claudianus

There is self pride, false pride, pride and prejudice; and there is pride of lions. Various types of pride include, school pride, national pride, community and caste pride, gender pride and other sorts of group based pride, even gay pride. Latin, superbia or hubris is considered, may be, most serious of the seven deadly sins. This means desire to be more important and attractive than others, remember the male peacock strut.

Tendency in the aforesaid is excessive love of self and failing to acknowledge others' work. One needs to be reminded, there is someone less fortunate out there and that keeps one humble.

Recognize distinctly the two faces of pride. One is hubris—excessive pride that veers into self aggrandizement, as also expressions of arrogance, grandiosity and superiority.

Says Tracy, it is wrong to say after achievement 'I am a great person".

The other side reflects achievement and mastery—"I worked really hard and deserve that praise." Still others may appreciate a larger degree of humility after achievement.

"Hubristic pride is associated with narcissism; one would be arrogant, conceited and egotistical leading to inter-personal conflict. Authentic pride is associated with, achieving, accomplishment, being productive, confident, fulfilled.

Low self esteem is an emotion contrary to pride. A balance with the latter would correct the former deficiency. Pride is different from primary emotions like joy and fear. Pride is categorized as a 'self-conscious emotion' which develops out of social interaction with others. "Authentic pride would motivate behavior geared towards long term status attainment," says Tracy, "whereas hubristic pride provides a 'short-cut' solution, granting status that is more immediate but fleeting and in some cases unwarranted."

Pride as an emotion plays a critical role for people reinforcing pro-social behavior, such as care-giving and achievement.

Feelings of pride may boost self-esteem, alerting the individual that he or she is valued by others. They (the pride-affected persons) are drawing attention and alerting their social group that they merit increased acceptance and status.

The above observations are based on research work by Jessica Tracy, an assistant Professor of Psychology at the University of British Columbia.

Following is another dimension on the subject with leaning towards ancient Indian Philosophy, by Vishal Arora.

Truly, it is ignorance to take the credit for one's accomplishments. For, achievements in life ought to humble us before God, who is the source of all good things.

Save and nurture self-esteem

> No one can make you feel inferior without your consent.
>
> **—*Eleaner Roosevelt***

Therefore take care to conserve and nurture self-esteem. The back-up of one's esteem makes one feel worthy and capable of meeting the challenges of life. It is as essential to mind as the blood and muscles to the body. Primarily it is the esteem which kicks up the thought and confidence to act.

"Yes, I can", springs up from the foundation of esteem whereupon stands the confidence to do and to contribute to life.

Situations in life provide opportunities to test one's self-esteem. It may happen that you are on your knees, having got an unexpected jerk. The game of life is not going to keep you always on the winning side. The sportsman's attitude of looking forward to another game, another day, arises from the realization that "I am esteemed self of the core of my being, I remain now and here-after."

An excellent quote from Cherie carter-scott follows. Remind yourself often that self-esteem is ephemeral. You will have it, lose it, cultivate it, nurture it, and be forced to build it over and over again.

It is not something to be achieved and preserved, but rather a lifelong process to be explored and cultivated. Where do your feelings of worthiness stem from? **Search to discover** the pathway to that source, for you will need to re-visit that source again and again throughout your life-time. When you can easily find your way to the core of your essential value, then know you have learned this lesson. We must acknowledge that we do not even have any considerable control over how long we will live, or what our circumstances will be like tomorrow.

In fact, we can't boast of the ability to work hard and achieve excellence and qualities of character; like honesty, will-power, and determination, which merely reflect in us the nature of our Creator. Besides, God has so made us that the first thing we learn is to depend on others. But when we "grow up" we often forget we depended on our parents and others.

Therefore, let us not be like a child who, proudly waving a paper, once cried, "Look, I wrote my name all by myself!" while her mum and dad smiled at each other over the childish pride of their child. Let us grow up.

Contra to pride cultivate decency

Also because decency is a secret of spirituality. When one tries to be decent, pride is curbed automatically. Decency is in itself a criterion of democracy.

The right to think as we wish is one of the prerogatives of democracy. Theists and atheists have existed since time immemorial and secular philosophies underline the democratic process, which potentially allow for all viewpoints to coexist.

Freedom means respect for worship in any form, be it through Hinduism, Christianity, Islam or others—or the right to be a non-believer.

If a wide range of devotional attitudes and lifestyles is encouraged and allowed to flourish, with improper behavior energetically restricted, citizens will be unafraid, safe and happy. Beyond mere tolerance and narrow-minded religiosity lies a land of peace and freedom. The thoughts stem from Mukunda Goswami and they encompass Pride vs. decency in a broad spectrum.

Transforming personality through sincere sadhna

The Jainas use the term *pratikramana* (withdrawal) with reference to the past, *pratyakhyana* (renunciation) with reference to the future and *alocana* (introspection) with reference to the present. Patanjali, the author of the *Yoga Sutras,* says that mysteries (siddhi, super-natural power), which are likely to happen with oneself, should be avoided as they may hinder the progress towards realization.

One should resolve to act self-watch-fully at least for an hour or two every day. The practioner should walk or stand still with the consciousness that he is standing or walking. The mind and actions should go together. The integration of personality is impossible without such a conscious attitude.

The development of the sense of equanimity means the purity of knowledge. This is the initial process of the transformation of personality. The above is a quote from Acharya Mahaprajna.

Ego and Ignorance can give way to humility

True humility does not come easy, for while it is possible to control our craving for food and even rid ourselves of addiction to substances, it is extremely difficult to subdue our ego.

Cultivating humility is to see the Supreme residing in each and every living entity and to treat everyone equally.

One day, after bathing in the Ganga, while making his way to the Sri Vishvanatha temple at Kashi, Shankaracharya saw a sweeper, broom under his arm, coming from the opposite direction along the same path. Succumbing to long-standing tradition, the Brahmin in Shankara spontaneously called out to the sweeper, "Move away. Move away". The sweeper, however, stood his ground and gently asked Shankara, "Is there difference in the space in a golden pot and the space in a mud pot? Is there difference in the one Consciousness (God) that is in the hearts of each living entity?" Shankara understood at once that the sweeper was reminding him that within the chaste Brahmin and the sweeper reside the same Brahmn (a.k.a. consciousness. 'chaitanya', soul, 'atman') and, therefore, Shankara was, in reality, the same as him, the difference being only in outer appearance.

One good method of cultivating humility is to see the one God residing in each and every living entity and to treat everyone equally. So relates Parmarthi Raina.

Humility in behavior builds mutual strength

Co-operation is the key. If there is to be such a thing as a worldwide 'human family,' working together for the common good has to be more than mere formality.

Carrying each other's burdens is part of love. The ability to trust comes from practical experience, and from being trusted. There are no shortcuts.

Another time-honoured phrase is *Bhava-grahi-janardana*. This refers to accepting another's good intentions and presuming that his or her faults will be overcome in the end. It also means combining abilities and working as a team.

May be this is overly optimistic and part of the world-through-rose-coloured-spectacles syndrome, but if reality checks are on board, then we can risk such leaps of faith.

Bill Gates' philanthropic investment in this country can be seen, among other things, as a significant gesture towards harmonizing the world's two largest democracies.

Leaders of nations can make a conscious effort to work together, or at least encourage their respective entrepreneurs to do so.

Integrating the wealth of India's culture with the strength of American technological progress can benefit millions. As the eternal children of a very rich Father, our horizons are virtually unlimited. The hope, as such, is expressed by Mukund Goswami.

Better to stop craving for Appreciation

Appreciation and frustration, the two may seem unconnected but the fact is that they are interconnected in a very subtle way. If we try for the first, the second is bound to come by. Whenever we do something commendable, we want appreciation from our relatives, society and peers for that work.

If we succeed in getting appreciation, we are happy. But unfortunately, if society does not appreciate our efforts, frustration entraps us and pushes us into the deep gorge of depression. This is disastrous. We should try to avoid it as far as possible.

You are not the only person on this earth who is not getting appreciation for efforts put in. So, being frustrated is not the solution to this problem. The actual way out is to do away with the scale of social appreciation and leave aside the battle for credit. As a famous proverb says "God does His biggest works through that person who does not care about taking credit." So the best thing is to kill the wish to be appreciated. And you'll never be frustrated. These thoughts are credited to Rajeev Prashar.

Be on the foundation of spirituality to be a good human being

Following is an extra-ordinary quote on the topic from Hemprabha Chauhan.

In an environment of wealth, power and pleasure, man is still listless and empty. He is full of tension and sorrow, doubt and uncertainty, all the time. Though he is aware of the artificiality of his mode of living, he is aiming at material prosperity, name and fame.

A happy man is still smitten by boredom arising from the limitations of his sense-bound achievements. He keeps wanting because he is not inwardly satisfied. The constant thought of material possessions, products and abnormal mental states, exerts a degenerating influence upon the soul.

Sensual desires are insatiable and the means of their fulfillment inadequate. As long as he looks upon pleasures and possessions as the primary objectives of life, he cannot be free of emotional attachment to them.

One who is attached to riches will have the fear of losing them and will constantly think of their care and, consequently, worry about them.

Svetasvatara Upanishad predicts that even though man may roll up space like a piece of leather, still there will be no end of sorrow for him without the realization of the luminous one within i.e., his 'self'. True happiness cannot be found in perishable things. It is found only in union with the Supreme. Bhagawad Gita says a wise man moves among the objects of senses free from love and hatred, keeping a tranquil state of mind absolutely controlled by his true self. But man is always in conflict between the divine and the undivine in him and unable to distinguish right from wrong.

According to the Yoga-Sutra Bhasya the stream of mind flows in two directions one leading to virtue and the other to vice. To overcome the conflict, man should take the help of religion or the path of realization.

When we live the life of spirituality, strength comes to us, our consciousness begins to expand, sympathies grow and widen and we become better human beings.

Life needs to be Harmonious

One is not in harmony if one does not know how to handle one's mind. An undisciplined mind can treat a gift as a curse.

Mind filled with ignorance creates a hell out of heaven and thus there is no harmony in life. How does one train one's mind? Just like how a dog is trained. It is given simple command, of firm 'yes' and 'no'. Untrained dog can be a nuisance at home. Whenever your mind worries or gets hurt, just say, 'No' to the mind, and then slowly the mind stops worrying. Worry is like a rocking chair that keeps you busy but leads you nowhere.

There is an invisible world of thoughts, emotions, likes and dislikes. The objective world has its reality and the subjective world has its own reality. To observe the self is self-observation. Self-change will make all the difference in one's life. This, as expressed by Swami Sukhabodhananda.

Forgiveness and peace from spirituality

Attaining peace is not easy. The hardest step towards peace is the first step, forgiveness. We must learn to forget the past and forgive our enemies. How can we take that first step? How can we cleanse ourselves of anger and hatred, and replace them with love and forgiveness? One solution has worked through the ages. Compassion, forgiveness and peace can be ours through spirituality. Spirituality is the recognition that our true self is our soul. It is recognizing that our soul is one with God. It is realizing that we are not merely our body and mind but a soul that inhabits the body.

When we develop this angle of vision, we no longer see through the eyes of prejudice and discrimination. We start feeling like we are all connected at the level of the soul.

When we experience this unity and collectedness, we start caring about each other. Aforesaid expressed by Rajinder Singh ji Maharaj.

We have to keep the hubris face of Ego at a distance. Certain values have to be conscientiously appended to the performing Ego. The irritating barbs of Ego are mellowed once Ego behaves lovingly. Love is personal as well as universal.

Following valued expressions have come about a decade ago from the noble soul of Sri Satya Sai Baba as follows.

Forgive and forget, pardon, forbearance, known as 'Kshma' in Hindi

Sentiment to condone, compassion, forbearance, has been recommended by even modern-day saints like Dalai Lama as one of the top virtues. This approach assumes that the person who is condoning a wrong doing on the part of another is sympathetic to the other person as a human soul. The giver, rather than being antagonized prefers in his mental calculation to let the receiver go without any punishment. As soon as one makes an effort to uplift his soul, he picks-up Love as a boon, as a gift from the son of God. It is for the whole world from Lord Christ. It is the virtue to be practiced by all human beings. Love flows from the divine and it is divine to practice it. One of the widely known saints from India, Shri Satya Sai Baba, in most of his discourses emphasizes the need to expand the cycle of Love to as large a radius as possible. Love to be meaningful has to be devoid of any selfishness. Actually, to be effective, Love rests upon self-sacrifice.

In this phenomenal world, the requirements necessary for life, say, to earn for your meals, for clothing and a roof on your head to begin with and all the rest which has to follow later, cause one to act and react for the sake of oneself and the family. In the struggle of fittest to survive, attitudes of selfishness and hatred etc. are difficult to avoid.

We have to understand the concept of KSHAMA at this stage as having a wider content than the English counterpart. This concept must not be understood as any sign of weakness in the face of grave offence or an absolutely unethical behavior pattern for which the correctional mode has to be adopted by way of punishment.

One can remember a small incident often portrayed in the films where a poor child runs across the road and pavement at break-neck speed just to steal a loaf of bread. He has been seen to be handed over to the police and being scolded and punished. This could make him a hardened criminal. On the other hand after catching the child by the wrist, the shopkeeper asked him the reason. The child stated that his old mother was on the sick bed and hungry. There was no one to pay for the bread, hence the theft. The shopkeeper advised him the obvious moral principle to be kept in view and happily gave him the bread as also told him to come later in case of absolute need. The child would learn to live as a compassionate human being. This is Kshama meaning some more than condonation. Kshama thus means more than forgiveness or to pardon or to just overlook.

To acquire Love as a characteristic of your character, it is necessary to imbibe Kshama in your attitude to face relative problems. Attempt must be made by all sensible individuals to cultivate this noble quality. One's own efforts are the prime engine to face difficulties of all kinds without bowing before the anxieties. The sufferings, sorrow and the opposite thereof, the pleasures are God given. To stand on the platform of equanimity is indeed difficult but more than worthwhile. He is great, who treats pain and pleasure equally in the two pans of the scale.

Man becomes more liable to various evil tendencies such as hatred and jealousy if Kshama is not acquired. To live with the former is to live with a disease. Like individuals if nations and their governments have compassion, they would come to terms across the table instead of going to war with each other.

CHAPTER – 6

NOTHINGNESS—
THE ULTIMATE REALITY

Nothingness, in between the planets is much larger. Birth and Death of Universe not cognizable.

As everyone realizes sometime or the other in life, all that has been achieved in this world has to be left here itself. One has personally no lien on one's own creations. How this shall be used or get destroyed one never comes to know when one has passed away from this changing world.

Howsoever strange it may appear but one does come to realize that one shall be no more in this world. Queer are the ways in which one may depart from this body, in childhood, young age or in the older years. The death may come in a prolonged painful fashion, by sickness, suddenly or by accident. A human being starts making efforts for Education, for one's career and for a married settled life.

There is a period when one may be lost in enjoyment for oneself. Equally likely that one may seriously devote oneself for the soundness and prosperity of one's progeny. Toil, more toil has to create weariness of mind and physique, deterioration of the organs of the body, an organic product destined to become useless stage by stage.

Brain is inquisitive. The mind wants to know as to what is the substance of life. If all will be lost with the loss of perception what is the use of toiling all one life. The eternal question arises as to what is the reality of this world. It is

ALBERT EINSTEIN

BIRTH : March 14, 1879
DEATH : April 17, 1955
"My religion consists of a humble admiration of the illimitable superior spirit who reveals Himself in the slight details we are able to perceive with our frail and feeble mind."

worthwhile to delve into the philosophies of different religions, modern thinkers and post-modern thinkers on the subject. According to the Upanishads (Hindu philosophy) the Ultimate Reality is **Brahman**. It (neuter gender) is at the origin of any physical, moral or spiritual activity (see also Brihadaranyaka Up. 4, 1-2; Chandogya Up. 3, 18, 1-6; Taittiriya Up. 2,6; 3, 1). Paradoxically, Brahman has two aspects: immanent, or manifested, and transcendent, or unmanifested. For a better understanding of this concept, we can compare it to the "Big Bang" theory of the origin of the universe. The point of infinite mass out of which all celestial bodies are said to have originated, according to the astronomic theory, has its ideological correspondence with the unmanifested Brahman of Hindu cosmogony. However, in the manifestation of Brahman, the product is not only matter, but also living beings, gods and humans. The cause of the manifestation process is Brahman's desire to be multiplied: "Let me become many, let me be born" (Taittiriya Up. 2,6,1).

(However, in a pantheistic context, this is a strange and contradictory idea, because the impersonal being cannot have desires. Probably a more accurate term would have been that of necessity of becoming manifested.) After the manifestation is completed, all its products tend to return to the initial state of unmanifestation, evolving from one level of manifestation to another. Then another manifestation will occur.

Samkhya and Yoga are two of the six Hindu orthodox schools *(darshana)* developed in the post-Upanishadic period. As most of their metaphysical basis is common, in the absence of any supplementary explanation, what is mentioned here is valid for both schools.

The world and individual beings came into existence as a result of the disturbance of the initial state of equilibrium between the three *gunas* properties, qualities (characteristics). Any known form in which we see the world manifested is generated by the participation of a certain proportion of the three *gunas*. The categories of *prakriti's* manifestation are, in hierarchical order, as follows:

1. Mahat, the first product of manifestation, considered to be a mass of pure energy which

appeared as a result of the *guna sattva* domination. Its psychic aspect is the intellect, buddhi.

2. From *mahat* evolves *ahamkara*, the principle of individuation (the sense for the *I*).

3. After producing **ahamkara**, (Ego, realization of (*I/me*) the evolutionary process takes two courses of action. Under the influence of the *guna sattva*, are produced the psychical evolutes: mind (manas), the five cognitive sense organs (sight, hearing, touch, taste and smell) and five associated abilities (speech, movement, prehension, excretion and reproduction). Under the influence of the *guna tamas* are produced the physical evolutes: the five subtle essences (the essences of colour, sound, touch, taste and smell) and the five gross elements, which emerge from the essence (the five fundamental elements in Hindu cosmology—earth, water, air, fire and ether). The *guna rajas* provides the force required for this manifestation.

Shiva and *Paarvati* together, *Ardhanariswara*, half woman and half man in their primordial unity form the beginning of this universe, as per *Tantrism* and *Hatha Yoga*. This concept is synchronous with the concept of *Bramha*. Lord Shiva decided to separate from his divine consort, also known as *Shakti*. The scripture, *Shiva Samhita*, states as follows in 1, 92

The spirit that is Shiva combined with the matter i.e. *Shakti*. By the intermingling of the two, the variety which we know as Universe, moving and the non-moving, living and the life-less were created. As per the Vedic pantheon *Shakti* is the Mother Goddess of land fertility and life. The same manifestation of the Absoluter in creation is presented in Shiva *Samhita* 1,52;69-77.

THE ULTIMATE REALITY IN BUDDHISM is nothing but a transcendent truth, which governs human life. This view point was brought forth by Buddha in the 6th century B.C. The concept of God is neither worshipped nor rejected.

As per the conservative school Gods were not considered as the basis for morality nor were the givers of happiness. They were temporary beings who attained heaven using the same virtues as any human disciple. SO THE IMPORTANCE IS GIVEN TO HUMAN VIRTUES, as enunciated in the speeches of the Buddha. This is the view point of the Therwada school which claims to have guarded the unaltered message of the founder.

The later schools viz. Mahayana Buddhism upheld a strong devotional trend which was reconciled with the concept of emptiness. The Yogacharya School, in the 5th century A.D., propounded the concept of three bodies of Buddha known as TRIKAYA. First one is called the DHARMAKAYA, the essential body of Buddha representing the emptiness itself i.e. the ultimate truth that governs the world. The other two bodies are for the attainment of Nirvana (no birth and no death location). Lower one in the table, Dharmakaya is formed by the two, one of which is Sambhogkaya, the body of enjoyment. It is here in their Pure Lands where they preach Mahayana doctrine to the Buddhas reborn here. The physical body of Siddhartha Gautama is the third body of Buddha, the NIRMANKAYA. This was the incarnation in this world for the benefit of mankind, unable to attain the Pure Land, the most ignorant and the weak. According to the traditional view he was a physical being, the founder of four noble truths and the first human that reached NIRVANA. In Mahayana Buddhism he is considered to be one of the many Buddhas, the compassionate beings that help other humans to find liberation.

TAOISM AND CONFUCIANISM

If Nothingness is deceptive to understand, TAO is equally unfathomable. Lao Tse was the founder of Taoism in China in the sixth century B.C. He has put down his writings under the title Tao-te-Ching where he has stated that the creative principle of the universe is its eternal truth. It is unchangeable and in continuation forever. This is stated to be an impulse which gives birth to all forms of living beings and heredity thereof. To the extent that this truth is recognized as an impulse, it is a divine form of power.

Lao Tse has stated, of course poetically in his poem that before the existence of heaven and earth (i.e. universe) there was something without any form or sound, it would neither depend on anything and would not change its nature, it could not be understood by differentiation and yet was complete in itself. Lao Tse further states that the impulse is operating everywhere and does not get endangered from anywhere. It has to be considered the mother of universe. Lao Tse does not know its name, he calls it TAO.

Other commentators have expressed that this philosophy is akin to the Brahminic Philosophy of Hinduism or what is known as Dharmakaya in Buddhism. Everything that take shape or gains a form originates from TAO. Lao Tse expresses poetically that all things from the seeding onwards, growth and decay included, have to ultimately return to their source of origin which is TAO.

The flow of nature from the seed to roots, trunk, leaves, flowers and fruit, is natural, the passage is smooth and peaceful. Like the two sides to a coin, two facets accomplish the objective and products of TAO. Lao Tse names the two complementary modes of Tao's functioning as Yin and Yang. The two are distinguished as the feminine principle of potency, regression and darkness named as YIN. The other half, the male principle, represents enlightenment, progressive movement and power of positivity, named as Yang. The two basics mix with each other in varying proportions, act as the main portions and as well as the catalysts for the resultant product. The product could also be abstract like an idea or the sentiments formulated. Lao Tse explains that all forms of existence, be it humans or their Gods receive their non-permanent existence from Tao.

THE THREE MAJOR MONOLITHIC RELIGIONS—JUDAISM, CHRISTIANITY AND ISLAM codify the following;

Here the God is personal who revealed himself through the story of Jewish people. This is found in the scriptures called Torah by the Jews and Old Testament by the Christians. In the very beginning of the Old Testament, God is presented as creating the universe out of nothingness. This is dissimilar to the process adopted by Bramha or Indra of Hindu scriptures mentioned as creating the universe out of His own substance or out of a pre-existent matter.

This nothing has no ontological status as it is not a primordial substance. Prior to creation nothing existed except God

The Psalms state:

In the beginning you laid the foundations of earth, and the heavens are the work of your hands. They will perish but you remain; they will wear out like a garment. Like clothing you will change them and they will be discarded. But you remain the same, and your years will never end.

For a student of Spirituality, the similarity of the simile stated in the Old Testament and the one stated in Srimadbhagvad Gita cannot go unnoticed The literal translation of the verse 2.22 of Gita is:-

22. As a person puts on new garments, giving up old ones, similarly the soul accepts new material body, giving up the old ones which are worn out or are useless for any other causes.

While the Old Testament explains the dissolution of the universe thro' the above simile and concludes the continuation of Spirit or the Super soul, the Gita concludes the eternal continuation of individual soul and destruction of the material body from time to time.

God is a personal being as per the book of Genesis. Creation is there because of an act of love, it is an act intended and completed by the creator. This differs from the Bramha of Hinduism, as perceived by the western writers, as this ultimate reality was incomplete without its manifestation in multiplicity.

GOD OF CHRISTIANITY

Christianity believes in a God which apart from being personal exists triumvirate, as Father God, the Son of God and the Holy Spirit. He has no beginning. He is not the primordial impersonal BEING (Bramha) of Hinduism as an abode of Omniscience, Omnipotence and Omnipresence.

Christianity believes that the Holy Trinity should be understood neither as a sum of three Gods (tri-theism) nor as a personal God that assumes successively three distinct forms. God's being does not exist outside the three entities, but only as Father, Son and the Holy Spirit,. There exists no ultimate reality beyond or above the Holy Trinity.

The God of The Bible admits no deeper ultimate reality beyond Himself

I AM THE FIRST AND I AM THE LAST, APART FROM ME THERE IS NO OTHER GOD. (Isaiah 44.6)

It was in the 6th Century A.D. that the other great monotheistic religion of the world, Islam was founded. Prophet Muhammad was the founder. Allah is the God of Islam. The reverred religious book Quran Sharif recognizes Allah as a transcendent and almighty being that is eternal. He is the supreme one. All beseech Him, He neither begets nor was begotten, as mentioned in 112th Surah in the Quran. Allah appears to have the attributes of God as Father of The Old Testament. Obviously the western writers observe the influence of the Old Testament on the Quran. While comparing the religions it may be kept in mind that as per Islam, Triune God of Christianity is considered to be heresy, both in Judaism and Islam.

Comparison of different religions of the world, in their different ways expounds the creator and the creation of Universe. Positions taken by the different religions are hardly reconcilable. Creation of the Universe is interesting from the point of view of the role of NOTHINGNESS from the very start of this rigmarole of material and immaterial objects and abstractions that we see around us. The beginning of the Universe may have some meaning for the end of this universe as and when it befalls our individual consciousness. The believers who wish to surmount the concept of ultimate NOTHINGNESS of life have a liking to take refuge in their respective faiths, Gods and spirituality thereof. Justification of this approach or otherwise, is a vast subject to be dealt with elsewhere.

Philosophers versus Physicists.

The philosophers are very verbose. For a commoner they are not easy to comprehend. Well explained religious texts are more likely to explain a beneficial meaning of life. We grasp the world around us with our consciousness. We are materially conscious by our perception. Our instincts boot our senses and we happen to perceive. That is our faculty of perception, say, part one of our consciousness. Then there is part two of perception which is beyond our cognitive capacity. Here we close our eyes, be at peace with ourselves in a comfortable position, and ask ourselves, as a saint Maharishi Raman says, "Who am I". By introspection we try to understand our consciousness.

The philosopher critically thinks that natural phenomena are explained by theory of physics. To him consciousness is also a natural phenomenon so this should also be explained equally.

This does not happen. Biology explains what life is and its evolvement. Neurology explains the functioning of brain, process of learning and memory but it does not explain as to what electrochemical reactions cause the experience of consciousness. Well then the scientific theory is incomplete because it does not explain consciousness. We can only be very sure of one's own existence, "I am very much here." Consciousness allows us to think, all else could be an illusion.

We find that consciousness has a number of functions such as, the sense of being 'I', thought, emotions (anger, sorrow, fear, jealousy and love etc.), with properties of unity, continuity which may arise from bodily experience or may be independent of the same at a higher level of thought processes. We are not clear whether it arises only from the brain or is related to other physiology as well. Cognition arises from memory, learning, speaking and reasoning. Perception is the physical process of knowing the world. Thought is the extended process of being conscious over a period of time. Now, who gives us the power to think. Is it that one thinks deeper than the other. In that case why the difference is there. Does the power of thought also empower us over material things in abstraction. How is the will power related to thought. Consciousness does have the power to relate to an eternity recognised as Super-consciousness.

"Mind is not big enough to understand mind". Philosopher Mc Guinn has been inspired by Bertrand Russel and Emanuel Kant to state that **consciousness is known by introspection**, as opposed to the physical world which is understood by the faculty of perception.

The relation between the two is as complex as between the brain and consciousness which is difficult to understand. Consciousness does not fall within the cognitive capacity of human brain. To supersede this thinking it needs to be stated that introspection is the route to comprehend consciousness. The limit of achievement relates to the effort and concentration thereof. Even the scientists constantly turn philosophical with their own language when they are seeking inspiration or trying to explain the meaning of their abstract findings; this was stated by Dr. Ullica Segerstrale, a social scientist at the Illinois Institute of Technology who has a background in physical chemistry.

Science has recently made **giant strides** in understanding the design of universe. Could it be that science makes us grasp the real content of universe as related to our life. Nothingness is fashionable again. When we last heard the notion, Jean—Paul Sartre, the French existentialist philosopher, was writing that "nothingness lies coiled in the heart of the being". He had published a good sized tome titled 'Being and Nothingness' in 1943.

Now the notion has cropped up outside of philosophical tracts as **physicists have identified** nothingness to be the central mystery of the origin and structure of universe. Physicists have been talking about a rather specific kind of nothingness. They want to know why the vast tracts of apparently empty space between the galaxies emerged with a strange sort of weight from the Big Bang that gave birth to the universe. Recent astronomical measurements have suggested that this "weight", which has a negative gravitational effect, is pushing the galaxies apart and accelerating the expansion of the universe.

But since the intergalactic vacuum, in effect, the deepest hole that nature can dig in material existence, it counts as NOTHINGNESS if anything does. **Einstein** first noticed that according to his theory of relativity, any weight of nothingness in space could push galaxies apart from one another, the effect that astronomers have recently observed.

Scientific Efforts to understand creation of Universe

Following is a sporadic approach by a humanist to get acquainted to the latest achievements of science by a lay man.

The physicists and related scientists are striving to reach, the first central particle or elementary nucleus from which the matter and the intervening gaps also called black holes came into being. With this objective in view, research work is going on at Geneva. Briefly, the laboratory has been given the name CERN. The laboratory, as per opinions of the research scientists announced in July 2012 that the ultimate particle was discovered and named **"Higgs Boson"**. In the initial fields of energy, called scalar fields, massive bundles of energy were identified. These appeared as a new kind of electrically neutral and unstable particles. This is being recognized as the elementary particle having a mass. The earlier theory of elementary particle was taken as a Standard Model which consisted of the electromagnetic force and the less familiar week nuclear force. These have been taken to provide the first step in the chain reactions which give the sun its energy.

The scientist Steven Weinberg stated that the weak and electromagnetic forces that became part of the standard model were verified when these particles were discovered at CERN in 1983-84. The subsequent discovery of Higgs Boson closes a gap in our understanding the laws of nature. The new particle was created by experimentation at CERN by collisions of protons (smallest of known particles, supposed to have first quantum of mass of matter) that occur at a rate of over a hundred million collisions per second. A simple fact about the magnitude of the experiment is that the collisions of the particles are made to happen in a 27 kilometer tunnel. All this has been stated to show that even at the cost of most elaborate scientific experimentation, we have understood the nature in a very small fraction. One is reminded of Newton who stated that (we, the scientists) are counting pebbles on the sea-shore.

All this effort explains 5% of the universe and as the astronomers say 95% of dark "matter" remains unexplained.

To understand life from the point of view of practicality, depending upon Philosophy, Religion or Science we have to come to a conclusion that we (the universe) are 'creatio ex nihilo', creation out of nothing from a primordial cause for matter that existed since eternity, say, space and time. Thomas Jay Oord (born 1965), a Christian Philosopher and theologian, argues that doctrine of creation 'ex nihilo' be abandoned. Oord speculates that God created our particular universe billions of years ago from primordial chaos.

The chaos did not predate God, however, for God would have created the chaotic elements as well. Oord suggests that God can create all things without creating from absolute nothingness. Okay then, for all we know, the universe may be heading for regression into eternity. How does our life proceed with us as we live through. Worth our while to consider the pros and cons.

EVEN THIS SHALL PASS AWAY

Life began in the **womb of the mother.** It took a shape having DNA and a physical form for all to see. The start from infancy, the cuddlesome looks and touch to match a feather, skin colour loveable to the culture where it belongs, progresses into growth. Everything changes and is left behind. Even the memory is not there in one's own mind. For oneself it is a story told by others. So, the infancy goes by into nothingness.

Adolescence is the period when one is conscious of the blood running in one's veins. For the first time one is coherently conscious of one's family and social surroundings. Life is to play and devoted to learning, whether automatic or under pressure. Discipline becomes a feature of life. Feelings, sentiments arise to awaken pleasure, anger, sorrow, affection, hatred and such other psychological features, in a more and more cognizable manner as the years go by. Later in life, memory reminds one of the loves' labour lost in that age. Attachment to friends, girls or boys of pre-teenage, of the teens, has a lingering flavour fading away into the years. Rarely and luckily some may be retained in the later years but the relations get drastically changed.

Teenage gives a character, ways of conduct, formative personality melts into the dashing years of youth. Teenage is gone into Nothingness.

A very valuable period of life comes by. **Schooling** happens; the class mates, teachers, the school surroundings, even the class rooms, canteen, the play grounds, play things, ladders, parallel bars, the parks, the prayer gatherings the school functions, varied personalities of the teachers, the grimaces of their faces and the formation of words as they were spoken, mimicry thereof by ourselves, the scolding, the cane when it used to be, the certificates, prizes and medals that were won and the effort put in, the welcome noise of clapping and cheers is all gone by. The passing years take away all hilariousness of the years and may give place to pensive memorial mood and tears some time. Gain is the education which takes on a changed shape in later years. What remains. All is lost in the past.

Youth goes through in agriculture or other familial surroundings where city life has not arrived. In the so called, civilised societies, life is lived through in cities, suburbs, in communes or in bungalows or palatial houses. The youth has an eye on some career or the other. Females may become house-wives, office employees or be on the upper rungs of the ladder up to the extent of 10 most powerful women in the world. Young men post-school would pass through Colleges and Universities, professional institutions, or maybe study privately to be on a job; highest to lowest strata thereof. May also be entrepreneurs or get into family businesses, small timers or empire builders.

Remember the excitement of first year in the College or the final farewells and convocations. Hours at the class rooms, laboratories, fields of research, in house training and duties, exchange visit programmes, national and international are gone by into the hands-on-job which is always Management of some sort. It could also be and mostly happens in today's fast world that the stress and strain, the consistency of flying around or just the day-night forceps of work tears down the family life or the fabric of health.Except for the unfortunate ones left behind in pecuniary despondence, very many may end up on cushions of comfort.

Before reaching the middle-age, youth loves to experiment with the most basic carnal instinct of sex. Very personal matter whether one manages to have many friends before marriage, or likes to be a virgin till marriage. Relations outside marriage may be considered taboo or 'chaltahai'. The age of sexual activity may reach exhausting levels at sixty, seventy or eighty but resignation, exhaustion or exasperation has to set in. After all, the good things must have an ending. One may come across couples, **made for each other** and those who lived happily together ever after. Seemingly, such smooth sailing is fortunate. Mostly, husband and wife have to rear a family in a spirit of mutual closeness, an adjustment of give and take, an attitude of mutual help, affection, friendliness and occasional noise arising as of articles hitting each other when they are too close. Planned or unplanned, the children join the stock of population because the old ones have to go, new ones have to grow and thus the universal continuity is maintained.

The stream keeps on flowing into the sea of Nothingness.

Old age is there to prove what this chapter intends to convey. The family is there for you if you are of any use to them. If you can give, you may be welcome. If you have to depend on them, you are likely to be abhorred. During your days if you have done your duty to them, in some societies, the younger folks of the family may look after you. In advanced societies, by force of circumstances or customarily, the chicks would fly away as soon as they learn to fly. The grip on whatever one has earned or built up gets more and more loosened till it is out of control. Admit this before time or when the doctor declares 'seizure of breath'.

In case **the departure** does not take place accidentally, the organic material starts decaying and it is very funny that some complication could start at any junction in any organ or multiple organs to form an excuse that now the case is beyond Doctors and perfectly on the mercy of the Almighty. The costliest effort by doctors in this world to tinker with something that is to happen by what is known as destiny, shall not succeed.

As per this writer, the universe was born out of Nothingness, as soon as the eyes of an individual close finally, this Universe may be as true as a dream. All that one gains materially at the end is Nothingness. Faith is therefore necessary to give any meaning to the actions of a lifetime and righteousness thereof.

CHAPTER – 7

KARMA

Lord Krishna with king Arjuna. (5,000 yrs. B.C.) "You have a right to Karma but no right to the result thereof"

W **h a t e v e r** **one does** in a life time by thought, word or deed is Karma. Some of these are voluntary and some are i n v o l u n t a r y. There are these functions, essential for living like breathing, intake of water, eating food, excreting and sleeping etc. These functions involve nominal thought processes as a cause. However the modernity of our civilization has made even these thought processes as very elaborate. The voluntary actions start from, maybe some provocation. It is said every action has a reaction. Or the Karma may start from a brain wave, one's own thought provocation. How does a thought arise. A very abstract beginning, could be something from the womb (a seed from paternity or maternity), could be something in the DNA having a property to create a cause. More tangible are the physical and mental characteristics groomed in the family and the society. So, we know how Karma kicks off from infancy itself.

Everyone comes to recognize "I exist" (*Mein hoon*). No doubt about that, "I am now here".

All through the life, with the first beginning of awareness, "I" **becomes the prime mover.**

All actions get related to the primacy of myself. I want this or I do not want it. I like it or I dislike it. I would want to have this in future or that shall not be my cup of tea. This is my plan of action. I act for the other person's benefit for a reason that is close to my heart. Maybe I have a reason to act against someone or his interests. The thought processes or implementation into action thereof results into a bouquet of KARMA. This ties up the positives and negatives of action to cause a reaction sometime; only destiny knows, how, when and where. I guess there could be resultant fragrance or stink, now or in future or in the next life, if there is one.

The psychological foundations of the individual start getting laid from the day the suckling starts off the mother's breast. Makes a difference if the feeding was received alongside mother's cuddle. Likely that the learning to receive and give security starts from that stage. Hell'uva difference would be there in the child's make up if the parents would be bickering amongst themselves. The nature of daily life for the child is a major participant in the formation of foundations of Personality. A slap on the buttocks at an ill tempered moment causes pain. If done repeatedly, it would result in hardened attitude, possibly hatred. The quality of response for an action could be worse from such a child as against a better nurtured child. The Karma at the level of infancy is more of a matter of concern to the parents or those who are in direct contact with the child.

The bounce back of reactions after the child grows up would be a source of effect on those who rear up the child.

Child hood is like Monsoon is for the crop. Correct showers, my God! what difference they can make to the seeds in standing upright as green plants, flowering and yielding fruit. A child could grow up to become Mother Teresa, Vivekananda or Abdul Kalaam or like any of the international celebrities. After the mother, the family is the casting frame that gives shape to the product. The Father's profession (an unskilled worker, a factory worker, an educated office hand, a Doctor, a lawyer, or may be a politician) or the mother, whether she is just a lady at the home or an office goer, both would give different content to the mental make-up and stability of the child.

A child from the age of understanding, say when he or she starts speaking at the age of two to three, would have a sense of loss and irritation if the Mom is leaving the child un-comfortable in some way to depart for work timings from the home. Personalities of the parents as they appear and as they interact with the child give him a glimpse of something to be or may be even an ideal. It is in this sort of environment that promptings for 'Karma', the nature and directions of actions in daily life happen to take shape. This in brief is the germinating ground for KARMA, formed in part by heredity and in part by the PERSONALITY as formatted by family and society.

Childhood gets directed into learning, whether outside the school, in the community or by way of Schooling. This period is of boisterousness or of application of mind or a balance of play and study.

These are the formative years of life, of gaining knowledge and of gaining skills. Some utilize this period whole heartedly and the others take it easy. College days are advancement into the knowledge and society beyond the frontiers of School. At the University, it is a panorama to experiment and to perfect. Up to oneself in youth to spoil oneself or to gain a pedestal for achievement. One's 'Karma' could be a contribution to society by way of Management, scientific contribution, in engineering or Medical help against disease or plain assistance or service to the needy. As one grows to be aged, one's intellectual acumen and experience is likely to enrich the quality of life in the world.

Study of Sociology tells us that Family and Society are the prime movers for personality, playing upon the field provided by biology and heredity. No living being lives without action. Action is a concomitant of life. The reactions to action provide the food for thought as to the good and bad result thereof. We see in our daily life that a thief commits an action which benefits immediately. As soon as he is caught, he has to suffer punishment. We also see that a public servant benefits by unfair means, gets richer and richer. The thinker naturally infers that, judiciary being a replica of a natural function comes into play; the wrong-doer must face justice here and now or some other time. Hence the question, is there some time other than the present life when the cycle of justice involving some wrong-doing and retribution is completed; maybe next sequential life.

We are obliged to notice what light the wise men of the past have shed on this subject.

Our thoughts and acts as related to morality

An idea occurs to one's mind, it starts with a speck and germinates into a body and an end, which instigates an action. Any action would have a moral value while a routine action would be neutral vis-à-vis moral value. For the principle of Karma what should be of concern is whether the formulated idea had a positive or a negative value. It is assumed that this value also is either positively added or negatively detracted from one's abstract record. Of course the action when acted upon has a resultant moral value of more solid weight. It should be understood that what we think, speak or do now will shape our future. As an example if we cause hurt to any living being, we shall have to bear the consequence of the same in one of our lives, present or in the future. Remaining conscious of good principles of social life and retaining them in action, we shall beget positive consequences.

Re-birth as understood in Buddhism

Accordingly, the actions undertaken have consequences as a law of nature itself. Now, as one undertakes a deed, the result is bound to follow. No one knows as to Y (what?) is the result of action undertaken X. This has not been specified and if stated anywhere, at best this will be a conjecture. What is known is that the effect that follows, either of happiness or of sorrow shall follow in the next few hours, days, years or in the next life or still later. Buddhism does not believe in the existence of a permanent Self (or ATMA of Hinduism) that reincarnates from one life to another.

It however believes in five elements explaining Life as such; these elements constantly arise on account of functional cause-effect relation, while they actually are impermanent ('anitya'). It is said that the illusion of Self is caused on account of the conglomerate of these five elements. To name these, (1) the body which is ('rupa') the material form of the being, (2) Feeling ('Vedana'); these are the sensations that arise from the body's sense organs, (3) Cognition ('sanna') which is the process of classifying and demarcating experiences, (4) Mental Constructions ('sankhara'), the states that initiate action, and (5) Consciousness ('gnana') that is the sense of awareness of a sensory or mental object. These together form an aggregate ('skandha') which itself is in a constant process of transformation. Consciousness cannot be identified in Buddhism with Self or *ATMA* because the former is impermanent. However it is interesting to note that dictates of *KARMA* are believed into. The riders of *KARMA* are reincarnated into the next life not by anything akin to Self. The transportation has been explained with the example of lighting one candle with the other; there is no carrier but the object has been passed on. The understanding is that Buddhism acknowledges the need to relate the conditions in this life to the *KARMA* of the previous ones.

In Buddhism faith is not placed upon ATMA of Hinduism. Naturally re-incarnation of the soul or Atma is not recognized. Instead, the soul is considered as an illusion, which is caused because of inter-mixture of five elements of nature.

Namely, (1) *Rupa*—the form of the material or a living being (2) *Vedana*—the sense organs of the body giving rise to sense—responses (3) *Sanna*—this is a process which separates different experiences and puts them into demarcated groups. (4) *Sankhara*—this is a mental state which commences and controls an action, (5) *gnana*—this implies the capacity to be conscious. It is the power to be aware of a sensory or mental object. All of these elements get together and form what is known as *skandha*. This conglomerate is consistently in the process of change.

Noteworthy that consciousness of Buddhism is not to be mistaken for Atma or soul of Hinduism. It is also interesting that the principles of Karma are fully respected. The transfer of consequences of Karma is explained by a mode different to that of Hinduism. In the latter thought, the Atma carries with itself, into the next life, a number of subtle characteristics of the soul with itself as an aura into the next birth. In Buddhism this is explained as the lighting of another candle by one that is already lit up. It has to be observed that the result of Karma principles in Buddhism is the same as that in Hinduism.

NIRVANA is the ultimate aim of a human being, fully evolved with moral attainment. In Buddhism the concept means one who has fully exhausted the process of retribution as also enjoying the prize of all good that has been done in this life or many of the previous births. The Lord Christ attained Nirvana, the supreme attainment, on the Cross when he surrendered his life to His Father, God almighty.

One can easily draw a parallel with the MOKSHA of Hinduism, which also implies conquering of all the desires, the instincts by the seeker.

THE CONCEPT OF REINCARNATION OR REBIRTH IN CHRISTIANITY

Though the major Christian denominations reject the concept of reincarnation, a large number of Christians profess the belief. In a survey by the Pew Forum in 2009, 24% of American Christians expressed a belief in reincarnation. In a 1981 Survey in Europe 31% of regular churchgoing Catholics expressed a belief in reincarnation.

Geddes MacGregor, an Episcopalian priest who is Emeritus Distinguished Professor of Philosophy at the University of Southern California, Fellow of the Royal Society of Literature, a recipient of the California Literature Award (Gold Medal, non-fiction category), and the first holder of the Rufus Jones Chair in Philosophy and Religion at Bryn Mawr, demonstrates in his book *Reincarnation in Christianity: A New Vision of the Role of Rebirth in Christian Thought*, that Christian doctrine and reincarnation are not mutually exclusive belief.

It is commonplace these days to hear the word 'Karma' used in popular parlance. Broadly speaking' Karma could be translated as "as you sow so shall you reap" and this is how it is usually understood by the Christians. The word Karma in popular concept, underscores the idea that there is a universal law at work that we live in a just world and no action (or thought) is exempt from consequences. Many surveys show that an increasing percentage of Americans believe in Karma and its corollary, reincarnation.

While believing in the principle of Karma, not believing in life after life is not a possibility. The tenet of rebirth in Buddhism is expressed as Walking the Wheel of Life. Traversing through the life in SANSARA i.e. this life on this earth in this world. We all know that going through this world is a very testing affair. The principle on which this material world operates is Survival of the Fittest or Big fish eat small fish. While one is in action, the conscience becomes a prey to Greed, Jealousy, manipulation to make one's own advantage out of someone else's loss, passions, unethical commission or omission, as also actions of a violent nature. KARMA implies collection of the consequence of what one has done through this life or the previous ones. To extinguish these, one gains sorrow or happiness which is the retribution of Karma. Bauddha Bhikkus (followers of Buddhism, the seekers) are advised to enter the stream of Nirvana which is entered into after extinguishing all the accumulated Karma. Attainment of NIRVANA means relief from THE PAIN OF BEING BORN AND DYING, again and again. Getting away from the circle of Birth and Death.

There is a **growing swell of agreement** that God would certainly not condemn man to an eternal everlasting hell, because it would be out of character for a 'loving and all forgiving' God. On the surface this argument sounds noble and within God's character. However, we must not forget that the God of the Bible is a loving God but that He is likewise a just God who must punish sin (I Thess. 1:8-9, Heb. 9:27).

Re-birth, Resurrection and Re-incarnation.

A person after his demise presents himself, according to the Bible, on his judgement day to receive his direction to go to Heaven or on a larger probability, to be damned to Hell for the punishment against the committed sins. This, because the life time is one and he has to pay for his doings at the end of it, now. This follows the faith in resurrection. To embrace, Reincarnation appears better to the extent that it allows one to live more than one life on one's own terms for the sake of morally evolving oneself, possibly till an agreeable stage in the eyes of one's Lord. This is permitted by the religions who hold Re-birth as a believable dogma.

According to the Bible, Apostle Paul is a witness to the resurrection of Christ. The Son of God and other Apostles who were resurrected from their graves were known to be the first fruits of the Garden of God. Subsequently both, God and his Son had the power to recall the dead from their graves. They believed in the Truth of God and when resurrected they taught the others, the truth.The resurrected had different spans of time and out of them some were befitting to the thrones. CHRIST WAS THE FIRST ONE TO BE RESURRECTED AND THE CHANCE WAS THERE FOR THE OTHERS TO FOLLOW HIM.

Re-incarnation is favoured by the logic that one life is not sufficient for the salvation to be achieved. Many lives are needed or God is kind enough to give many opportunities to gain a standard of moral evolution. The science of the soul and salvation has to be studied and ingrained to gain divine following and divine qualities in a life of flesh and blood.

Contrarily, Hebrews 9/27 offers the other perspective that man has only one life time in which to get to the right side of God.

Philosophically a view point offered for one's embrace is that there is no moral judge and that GOD IS IMPERSONAL. Reincarnation therefore is the best possible pathway to improve physically, mentally and to evolve spiritually. Be there no moral judge, no judgement occurs, either for moral or for physical sin. It appears that in this case one is oneself the Guru and the disciple. To be watchful and to educate oneself for the moral pinnacle is a self-given directive as also the ultimate aim of life.

Re-incarnation provides for the fact that the vast suffering in the world does not agree with the known benevolence of God. He never imposes of His own accord, the witnessed kind of suffering on the mankind. This must be caused due to the accumulated Karma, good and bad, in the past lives. To live through one life only, for the sake of what had been lived in the past, is not judicially fair to the suffering. More lives and more chances are given to redeem the cause of suffering.

Jesus, by His death got his own salvation on the Cross by His work. To the re-incarnationist the work of Jesus opened the doors for his own salvation. He has to make efforts by himself to gain his salvation. Work of Jesus on the Cross provides a full force impetus to him to work for his salvation.

Man has to solve his own dilemma, it cannot be out-sourced. Salvation is achieved by his own works, rather than relying on the work of Jesus. According to the Scripture, salvation to be achieved through one's own works, is the only solution to the true God, God of the Bible.

REINCARNATION IN ISLAM

Reincarnation is refuted by all the main Monotheistic religions of the world. The reason for this is that it is against their basic teachings of a finite life for the human upon which he/she is judged and rewarded accordingly. If the human is to go through numerous lives, on which life is he/she to be judged? The first life? The last life? The Holy Quran, the last and proven word of God, unequivocally rejects this false religion of reincarnation.

"The Hindu belief in reincarnation is well known. But it is not known that the Koran refers as kafir (deviant) anyone who doesn't believe in the possibility of rebirth. Not many in India have perhaps come across the verses of the great mystic, Hazrat Jalal-ud-Deen Rumi, describing the process of evolution through reincarnation—from mineral and plant to animal and man and then to angelhood and beyond. Take the verses from the world famous Masnawi by Hazrat:

> *I died as mineral and became a plant,*
> *I died as plant and rose to animal,*
> *I died as animal and I was man.*
> *Why should I fear?*
> *When was I less by dying?*
> *Yet once more I shall die as man,*
>
> *To soar with angels blest;*
> *But even from angelhood I must pass on . . .*

Another great mystic, *Mansur al-Hallaj*, famous for his formulation, Anal Haq (I am the truth: Aham Brahmo Asmi) wrote:

Like the herbage
I have sprung up many a time.
On the banks of flowing rivers.
For a hundred thousand years
I have lived and worked
In every sort of body.

The Koran itself seems quite clear: "And you were dead, and He brought you back to life. And He shall cause you to die, bring you back to life, and in the end shall gather you unto Himself." (2:28). The words "you were dead" can only mean that they had lived before becoming dead. And the words "in the end shall gather you unto Himself" could very well mean the attainment of moksha (release) rather than an eternal life in heaven or hell. Those who disagree, however, contend that "dead" is very commonly used for non-living things. "It does not necessarily mean that you were alive before being a non-living thing or dead." (S Abdullah Tariq in Islamic Voice, February 2002)

Thus the debate goes on. One thing, however, is certain: most of the greatest saints Islam has produced believed in reincarnation and it does constitute a part of many Muslims' belief system. This is primarily caused by reluctance on the part of many Muslims to believe that God will merely reward or punish human beings on the basis of a lifetime in which they may not have received the guidance necessary to improve their conduct.

That God will just be reconciled to their being sent to an eternal life in heaven or hell without their being given another chance to improve themselves becomes a proposition difficult to believe." Reincarnation in Islam, Sultan Shahin, Asia Times Online, Dec 25, 2003

Karma in Hinduism

The concept of Karma *(Sanskrit)* or Kamma *(Pali)* had its origin in the Vedas and Upnishads. The early Upnishads are placed in the time period around 1500 BC. Karma is as integral to the embodied soul as gravity is to the cosmos. A human being's Personality is as much the product of Karma as its further creation in thought, vibration, action results into anything and everything that is known to be Karma. The principle, law and inevitability of Karma has been referred to in the Hindu scriptures i.e. Vedas, Upnishads, Mythologies viz. Puranas, Mahabharata, Bhagvadgita, various treatises, told and retold commented upon by seers, Rishis and Munis. The original concept of Karma was later enhanced by several other movements within the religion, notably Vedanta, Yoga and Tantra. This is a great philosophical nugget, the secret of which is available to the human beings for their comprehension. One has to be absolutely clear about the width and depth of the applicability of the all encompassing phenomenon that is Karma. Let us relate to the same in following paragraphs.

The being exists in time and space, in the cosmos that is governed by immutable laws of nature. Similar immutability is attributed to the cause and effect that creates Karma. All actions, thoughts and vibrations of any sort are governed by the law that demands perfect rebound.

All *'jiva-atmas'* (soul and its body) must have to perform Karma and have to experience it with the attributes. In this subtle system there are the components that perform, store and eventually bear what is resultant. There is of course the carrying system and carriers into the future, all related to the body and the soul.

TYPES OF THOUGHTS, ACTIONS AND OBJECTS

There are supposed to be three types of the above and all aspects related to life which falls under the demarcated three Types. Almost anything can be named to fall into one of the following three types. They are considered high and low against some measure of ethics and aesthetics.

SATTVIKA

Means truthful, pure something or quality that is more likely to make the path easier to realization of Truth. It is liked by a clear conscience; it is benevolent, philanthropic, simple, humble, not irritating, non-violent, clean in appearance, content and effect. There would be Sattvik, talk, action, clothes and food, not excessively spicy, surely not non-vegetarian. Not what is known as a life of 'wine and women'. This would give some idea of an ideal life of Sattvik Karma.

RAJASIK

A rich life lived on the basis of satisfaction of worldly wants. An average family man lives this type of life, though may be without riches. Gaudy, expensive garments and a gourmet's food, liquor and all that sets aside ethics for the sake of enjoyment would fall under this category.

Viewed against an inspection prism, this kind of life has a fifty-fifty chance of reaching Sattvika reservoir of Spirituality or going down this table towards the next lower classification of *TAAMASIKA*.

TAAMASIKA

A life wasted from spiritual view point. This is all that is known as bad from social as well as cultural standards. Habitual drunkards, womanizers, criminals, people with violent behaviour, those who are generally harmful to the family and to society would fall under this category. Obviously it is easier for a Rajasik person to move up to the Sattvik category. The chances of moving from the Taamasika to Sattvik category are rare. Taamasika habits etc. are advised to be totally avoided. Heavy drinking, smoking and drugs etc. are dominant examples of Taamasika nature.

GENERAL

What certain viewpoints may term 'destiny' or 'fate' is in actuality, according to the laws of Karma, the simple and neutral working of Karma. It could be likened to an Accounts Ledger, where there would be a credit or debit of good or bad Karma. Add to it the angle that, any action good or bad binds us to recurring cause and its effect; this could be mental, physical, light or acute, close or far removed, related to oneself or with a fall-out for the family. The effect is really too complex to explain. Beyond this is a too lofty an ideal, a stage to be craved for achieving the ultimate of human existence, to attain supreme consciousness, to escape the cycle of birth, death and rebirth.

One must transcend the knot of Karma, both good and bad. This method of transcendence is dealt with in different streams of Hinduism, Buddhism, Jainism and even in other faiths and philosophical systems as well. Now that the subject has reached this far, allow this writer to express that a desirable mode of life is to be Sattvik, have birth and rebirth to serve the needy, depressed and downtrodden, as is upheld by all Religions.

THREE KINDS OF KARMA

The span of time includes Past, Present and Future; kinds of Karma are identified accordingly.

PRARABDHA KARMA (Fatalist point of view)

The *'Karma-phala'* (fruits or consequences of action) of one life time do not get exhausted in the same life time. It is inevitable that they have to be lived through by the *'jiva'* (living being) who owned them in the first place. *'Karma-phala'* remains immutable. Consequentially the Karma travels as *'Samskara'*, an ethereal representation of the whole, to the next life, riding upon the soul as an integral property. One's likings, abilities, attitudes and inclinations are based upon the thoughts and actions of last life. This is a part of the basis in the next life, as a cause for the family where one takes birth, for the looks, the personality, the economic condition, the position in society, the various pleasures and pains that one suffers, so on and so forth.

SANCHITA KARMA (Collection of the past and present life)

Added on to what is carried from the last life is, what is acted upon or undergone in the present life.

'*Viveka*' or volition is the tool, meditation and '*dharmika*' (religious or ethical) practices are the instruments whereby severity of the effects of Karma can be ameliorated. Hindu system of Yoga and preachings by the Gurus can lead to such practices as may help towards alteration of the "*Karma-phala*". The '*gunas*', properties of life, earlier described as Sattvika, Rajasika and Taamasika have an alterable dynamics by virtue of application of mind and practice. As an example one could cite the case a person who is into Meditation and evolves into an improved and balanced life-style.

The net add-ons and the principal of Karma earned in the current life time has to be carried forth into the next life. There is an interesting analogy in Vedic lore. Imagine an archer about to shoot an arrow. The arrow that has already been shot and is travelling to its destination represents *Prarabdha Karma*; it is fate in action. The arrows stored in his quiver represent the Sanchita Karma, the accumulation so far. And the arrow that is ready to be shot from his bow is *Aagami* (forthcoming) *Karma* or *Kriyamaan Karma*. The archer has a sort of control over the arrows in his quiver *(Sanchit Karma)* and on the one that is about to be shot from his bow and he has no control over the one that has been shot. Likewise the individual has no control on *Prarabdha* while he could exercise his volition vis-a-vis *Sanchita and Aagami Karma.*

AAGAMI KARMA

This is the Karma of the present life and one may say that over this one has control in the sense of action ability of one's volition. One creates one's Karma in the present life for its own future as also to be gone through in the lives to come.

Question arises quite often, "Why do bad things happen to people who are so good in the present life time e.g. even the well known saints, Ramkrishna Paramhans who suffered from Cancer or Sai Baba of Shirdi who suffered from asthama." Suffering in the present life time is explained, as a result of Prarabdha Karma.

There is the good Karma and Bad Karma and the Mixed Karma.

Looking at the phenomenon in simple terms, all Karma has a relative perspective in that one Karma can have good result for one aspect and bad result for another. Therefore a performer has to keep watch that the consequence should do maximum good and minimum bad. In Hinduism, Karma works within a cyclical framework that sees the phenomenal universe being created and then eventually dissolved into itself. Karma is finally dissolved by the suggested ways or more often than not it perpetuates itself.

KARMA CLASSIFIED

Karma does allow for Divine Grace through intense devotion and love of God. Lord Krishna has advised in Geeta that one can transcend 'Karma-phala ', the fruits of action, and be liberated. Towards this end known as Moksha, one is aided by the love of God, His benevolence alone which has to be sought after by various means of Yoga. Yoga is no mysticism, it just means getting hitched, getting attached to Him by practising ethics as a Human being.

TRANSFER OF KARMA TO NEXT LIFE

To be aware of the mechanics of transfer of Karma to the next life let us understand the nature of our body. One is the 'Sthula Sharira' (Gross body), the other phase of the body is the *'Sukshma Sharira'* (Subtle Body). Very interesting to note that the body has a substance and aura of five sheaths. They are discerned as follows.

ANNA-MAYA KOSHA. (kosha = sheath)

In the material body the reigning elements are, earth, water and fire. From them we get food and drink which is digested by the fire of digestion and further converted into the body of food.

The nature provides by inheritance from the parents, the *'Indriyas'*, the organs of sense and the faculties of sense. In the gross body there are external *'koshas'*, viz. hair, blood, flesh, bone, muscle, marrow and of course the covering by way of skin. The organs of sense (Indriya) are of two kinds, viz. Jnanendriya or organs of sensation, through which knowledge of external world is obtained, namely ears, skin, eyes, tongue and nose. Karmendriyas or organs of action are, mouth, arms, legs and anus. Their functions are, speech, holding, walking excretion and procreation. This in short is the body that one has to leave on earth before proceeding to another life.

PRANA-MAYA KOSHA (The sheath of Breath).

This second sheath of breath or *'Prana'* manifests through air and ether. It would be good to understand that breath is the main force which the human being can use as a tool to connect with super-consciousness through the Yogic process of Pranayama leading to intense meditation. Breath is what connects life to body and breathing is a process that can be put to immense spiritual benefit. Prana as the sublime entity is illumined by the light of the un-known and un-realised Super-consciousness. Physically it functions through subtle breath or Prana-functions which are five-fold viz. inspiration and expiration, Udana is the ascending 'Vayu' (breath-air supplement), Apana is the downward force of Vayu, expelling wind, excrement, urine and semen. The 'Samana' or the equally collective Vayu conducts the food and blood etc. in the entire body, Vyana is a separate Vayu force effecting division and diffusion in the body.

These five forces cause respiration, digestion, circulation and excretion. Obviously, this all is consumed with the body in one life time.

MANO-MAYA, VIJNAN-MAYA AND ANAND-MAYA KOSHAS

The next two sheaths are the Mano-maya and Vijnan-maya Koshas. These two constitute the entity of the individual's subtle being called Antahkaran. The controlling and directing authority of the consciousness. It has the Mind with two aspects 'manas' and the 'buddhi', the first one is the direct registering station of the observation by the senses and the second one is the analyzing supervisor. The first part dwells on the certainty and uncertainty a.k.a. Sankalpa, Vikalpa; whether it is this or that. The second part decides, determines and cognizes, by application of intellect. All this happens on the platform of consciousness of Self i.e. the subjectiveness of oneself. This is known as 'Ahankara', i.e the realization, I AM. Mind in its wider sense raises for itself the subject of its thought; let us say to a higher level, this contemplation (*'Chinta'*) is done by Chitta, a faculty of Antahkaran. These are the functions, as we know, of the Consciousness, Ego to the extent of realisation of one's existence, Mind with its waves and the intellect that decides. The enduring entity that guides the subtle being Antahkaran is known as Chitta.

Anand-maya Kosha is the residence of Bliss. It remains to be attained in persistence while everyone has a possibility to taste it in a life-time. Soul is eternally in search of this treasure. Physical body and its Soul have three stages while living through life.

'Jaagrit Awastha', the state of being awake when we conduct all work in the external world. The state of Dream Sleep, *'Swapna Awastha'*, here mind is not registering fresh sensations but is still working on what has been recorded in the awakened state in a relevant or irrelevant fashion. This is a stage of objectification of visions perceived on the mind due to the perception of ideas that were latent. The third stage is that of *'Sushupti'*, or dreamless sleep when *'manas'* (observing mind) and *'buddhi'* (discerning capacity) is withdrawn and the preserved notion is "Happily I slept, I was not conscious of anything." This is an experience of the self being merged in the causal body. It is the nearest one gets to know the *'Samadhi Awastha'*. This feel of peaceful happiness is a glimpse into the bliss resulting from deep meditation known as *SAMADHI*. If one is fortunate one could come across in appropriate locales, a Sadhu sitting in *"Padmasana"* in a condition of Samadhi, usually a prolonged undisturbed posture. This state of mind, intellect and body merged into causal body in a blissful status is known as *'Turiya Awastha'*. Beyond these states, there is also a stage of total perfection which is not the subject matter of this treatise. The physical or gross body is called the *Sthula Sharira* which is left behind. The Subtle Body known as *Sukshma Sharira*, also called Linga-sharira or *Karan-sharira*, comprises ten *Indriyas, Manas, Ahankara, Buddhi* and five functions of *Prana*. The relevant Sukshma Sharira travels with the Soul at the time of Reincarnation. The subtle body contains in itself the cause of rebirth into the gross body when the period of reincarnation arrives. We have thus achieved some knowledge of the process by which the Karma is carried over to the next life.

CHAPTER – 8

LOVE

Jesus Christ

The acid test of our love for God is obedience to His Word.

I wish to quote two sayings of a Sufi saint of recent times, Sai Baba of Shirdi.

"Love and Service are two wings by which man can soar to higher levels of consciousness. If you have the spirit of Love and Service, divine grace will follow you like a shadow, wherever you may be."

"Share your love with birds, animals and fellow beings, Absolute love is true liberation."

Human personality is a social entity. It lives in love just as a fish lives in water. See love in a wider sense like a gesture of cognition, just a look with an attitude, an extended hand, an initiative to give and receive, familial and social interaction, and so one might as well be a log of wood without love.

The need to expect love at all times is so ingrained, obviously because one is so assured and habited of the warmth of love in the mother's womb. Probably that is why a human being keeps striving for material as well as psychological security, all one's life. It is love or its equivalent received that accords security to exist.

A smile is exchanged and we know the simple happiness of having met or the complexity of relations. A glance can mean so much more than what is apparent. The body language would show whether you may expect service to your wants or one has to ready oneself for an assignment. A hand-shake means both of us are there just for the pleasure of being together or to solve a problem which is an obstruction to our purpose which we love. Parents' love is the strongest of pillars to a balanced personality and contrarily parents' rejection can cause fathomless damage to the nature of developing persona of the child. A game played with love of knowing each other as a friend yields so much of satisfaction or is an introduction to the variety of inter-personal relations. If a teacher is able to gain from his ability, a regard that is a form of love, being educated is a pleasure to the student. Participation in activities like dramatics, lecture sessions, debate sessions and such other extra-curricular

Sai Baba of Shirdi
1836-1918
"If you look to me, I look to you. If you cast your burden on me, I shall surely bear it."

activities is a valuable step to mature a personality for useful contribution to the society.

An individual is a product of hereditary factors that provide the physique and its temperament, which forms the foundation.

Their constant interplay with the society, its sub-groups, the culture thereof including religious influence and the government policies define the uniqueness of individual personality. In all social relationships existence of Love can be discerned like warmth in a body that is alive. Whether it is functional or dormant but it is very much there.

The interaction of LOVE is one to one or many to one and vice-versa. Finally it is very charming either way, whether the meaning is worldly or divine. The way this word is loosely, used could just mean, "I love XYZ ice-cream". Then, there are the individuals and groups who for the love of a different dogma are ready to smash the 'establishment'. For the love of what, they know better, the human body would be trained to transform into a human bomb and blast other human beings into smithereens. A group would conspire to burn the other group travelling in a railway compartment for the love of their faith. A mob has individuals who form a mob for the love of retaliation and would burn up a colony of innocent civilians because they name God almighty in a different way which they happen to believe in. Love of faith can make a group so die hard that they would fly planes in a suicide attack to strike down sky-scraper buildings of a prosperous nation whose faith happens to be different to theirs. Look at this strife for love. Look at war being fought for the love of one's interest, part for self and part for a wider cause. In any case, what one destroys, is creation of nature.

Another angle, Love supposedly is used to create a new morality, abandoning the principles of goodness and moral standards in society. In the name of Love they use drugs and narcotics to bring them artificial pleasure during which they exploit the natural and innate instinct of sex.

Love of Christ

The word Love is used so loosely that it signifies to them anything other than its real meaning and content. The content of Love got perverted when it means nothing more than satisfaction to sexual arousal. Love in its very basic meaning is understood primarily in relationships between persons. It is an expression of ardent attachment through a refinement of human emotion. It is, in its genuineness, put across through devotion, loyalty, intimate knowledge and responsibility. Love is the total righteous understanding of a mutual relationship between persons. Love is not subjective; it is devoted to the object. It has intrinsic joy as its essentiality. If sorrow is experienced, it has as its cause, the separation from the object of Love.

It is true that in past centuries, Love has been exploited by individuals and groups, but it always was found that this kind of Love was wrong and needed correction and refinement. Love has had an ideal to keep progressing, refining, upgrading itself through the years in the expression of concern for all peoples. **The Christian concept of love** is mentioned in the divine declaration,

"You shall love the Lord your God with all your heart, and with all your soul, and with all your mind. This is the great and first commandment. And a second one is similar. You shall love your neighbor as yourself. (Matthew 22: 37-39 f). God is Love. God, as the source of Love, possesses great mercy and compassion. Out of Love God sent His only begotten Son, Jesus Christ to save mankind. Out of Love Christ humiliated Himself and even died on the Cross to atone for man's sins. Out of Love, Christ offers "fallen" man a second chance to attain his salvation through His church. Out of Love, God offers everlasting life to those who obey His commandments as His heirs. This is supreme Love, a Love for the man whom He created, even though He disobeyed Him through arrogance. The tender mercies of God for man whom He created are over all His great works. God reveals Himself to those who walk in His footsteps in the path of humble service to their neighbor. The profound message that permeates Scripture revolves around the love of God and love of man.

In Islam the concept of love is exemplified in the Love of God for the Prophet Muhammad and the Prophet's love for God. The prophet is known as 'Habib Ullah', the beloved of God. Over the centuries the Muslim saints have experienced divine love through this concept.

Human love for Allah, His creations, deeds and human beings play a crucial role in Islamic world view, especially in theology, ethics and mysticism. Indeed knowledge of religious truths builds up faith but is not reducible to knowledge alone. The belief and faith arise from commitment to the articles of faith and from the fact that one does not refuse to follow them. Faith is there when one loves the religious beliefs and not just by virtue of knowing them. Study of the Quran, its narrations ('hadiths') shows that the meritorious and ethical properties are to be loved and the converse is to be hated e.g. justice is to be loved and injustice is to be hated. Thus, one person may be loved for his good deeds and at the same time he may be hated for the bad deeds. Love and Hatred are like two sides to a coin, functionally for the sake of Allah. Islam recommends compassionate dealings and sincere relationships with others even if they do not believe in Islam or God.

Love of God has to be complete above all else. One should not think that one is directing the course of love. Love for God itself directs the course of your love. Love has to be unstinting as it was in the case of one of the earlier prophets, Noah. Inspite of the taunting and insults by locals as well derision for his family, Noah remained faithful and loyal to the words of God. He built a boat even though no clouds were to be seen anywhere. As per God's instructions he collected a pair of every animal. It did happen that the floods came and Noah's faith was proved true. No others could survive but the family of Noah. There were heavy rains for forty days and nights and everything was destroyed. The unshakeable faith In Him paid off.

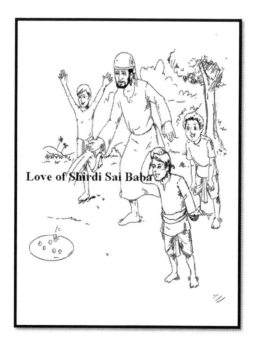

Love of Shirdi Sai Baba

The following narration is from the scriptures in the words of devotee Nasser Lallji (Mumbai). It is best if you put God's wishes before your own, and wonderful if both are one. In the Bible Hosea 6 v 6 "I don't want your sacrifice. I want your love. I don't want your offerings. I want you to know me." Says the Lord. Sai Baba of Shirdi (Indian saint of recent times) said, "Carry me in your hearts."

For our relationship with God to grow there is a responsibility to obey—not from a sense of fear but fear of hurting him. We know that he is our creator and that His purpose and plan for us is for our good. Our path, which is laid out before we are born is following our Karma. This cannot be changed, but it is our faith in our Creator born out of our love, that will guide us through unscathed and stand us in good stead in the future.

After the flood water had receded, God told Noah to enjoy the creation and replenish the earth. He was'nt told to follow the rituals but enjoy life. The steps of the godly were barely directed by the Lord. He delights in every detail of their lives." Psalm 37 v 23. God is pleased when we go about living our lives to please Him but this is only possible if we obey Him completely and that cannot come without trust, and that again can come only with faith, which is based upon love.

Prophet Abraham's belief in God came after much thought. In the Quran in Chapter 6 verse 75 (006.075) it is said "So also did we show Abraham the power of the laws of heavens that he might (with understanding) have certitude. When the night covered him over, He saw a star: He said, "This is my Lord." But when it set, "I love not those that set." (Again in Chapter 6 verse 76)

When he saw the moon rise in splendour, he said, "This is my Lord." But when the moon set, he said, "Unless the Lord (saves me), I shall surely be among those who go astray."

(Chapter 6 verse 77) When he saw the sun rising in splendor, he said, "This is my Lord, this is the greatest (of all)." But when the sun set, he said, I am indeed free from your (guilt) of giving partners to God." (Chapter 6 verse 78) "For me I have set my face, firmly and truly, towards Him, who created Heavens and Earth, and never shall I give partners to God. "(Chapter 6 verse 79) In these Chapters some light is thrown on the mental experience through which Abraham (peace be on him) passed in the beginning and which led him to an understanding of Truth before Prophethood was bestowed on him.

Certainly he was as familiar as anyone else with nightfall and ensuing daybreak. The Sun, the moon and stars, all had risen before his eyes in the past and disappeared from sight. But on one particular day his observation of a star was to stimulate his thinking in a direction and to lead him in the end to perceive the truth of God's oneness.

Prophet Abraham's faith was so perfect that even though thrown in a raging fire, he came out unscathed, just as Prophet Daniel remained alive in a den of hungry lions. Little wonder then that **Prophet Abraham is called** "Father of the prophets "by the Jews, Christians as well as Muslims.

TAOISM

For the love of life, your own self and the world around you, I find the following selected QUOTES FROM TAOISM very interesting to be kept in view.

Do you really want to be happy? You can begin by being appreciative of who you are and what you have got

1. Accept everything the way it is.
2. Do not seek pleasure for its own sake. Do not, under any circumstances, depend upon a partial feeling.
3. Think lightly of yourself and deeply of the world.
4. Be detached from desire lifelong.
5. Do not regret what you have done.
6. Never be jealous.
7. Never let yourself be saddened by a separation
8. Resentment and complaint are appropriate neither for oneself nor others
9. Do not let yourself be guided by a feeling of lust.
10. In all things, have no preference.
11. Be indifferent to where you live.
12. Do not pursue the taste of good food.
13. Do not hold on to possessions you no longer need.
14. Do not act following customary beliefs.
15. Do not collect weapons, or practice with weapons beyond what is useful.
16. Do not fear death.
17. Do not seek to possess goods or fiefs for your old age
18. Respect Buddha and the Gods without counting on their help.
19. You may abandon your body but preserve your honour
20. Never stray from the Way.

(These specified above are to be viewed against the intended context. Modern life would need adjustments without alteration of the basic ethical content.)

Those who do not know how to suffer are the worst of. There are times when the only correct thing we can do is to bear out our troubles until a better day.

Shape clay into a vessel, it is the space within that makes it useful.Cut doors and windows for a room: it is the holes that make it useful. Therefore benefit comes from what is there; usefulness from what is not there.

Grappling with fate is like meeting an expert wrestler; to escape, you have to accept the fall when you are thrown. The only thing that counts is, whether you get back up

WHO KNOWS WHAT IS GOOD OR BAD?

The Taoists realized that no single concept or value could be considered as absolute or superior. If being useful is beneficial, the being useless is also beneficial. The ease with which such opposites may change places is depicted in a Taoist story of a farmer whose horse ran away. His neighbor commiserated only to be told, "Who knows what is good or bad?" It was true. The next day the horse returned, bringing with it a drove of wild horses, it had befriended in his wanderings. The neighbor came over again, this time to congratulate over his windfall. He met with the same observation, "Who knows what is good or bad?" True this time too. Next day the farmer's son tried to ride one of the wild horses and fell off, breaking one leg. Back came the neighbor, this time with more commiserations, only to encounter for the third time, the same response, "Who knows what is good or bad?" And once again the farmer's point was well taken, for the following day soldiers came by commandeering for the army and because of his injury, the son was not drafted.

According to the Taoists, yang and yin, light and shadow, useful and useless are different aspects of the whole and the minute we choose one side blocking out the other; we upset the nature's balance. If we are to be whole and follow the way of nature, we must pursue the difficult process of embracing the opposites.

PRAYER

When you find yourself in one of those mystical/ devotional frames of mind or in an emergency and you feel you want to pray, then pray. Don't ever be ashamed to pray or feel prevented by thinking yourself to be unworthy in any way. Fact is whatever terrible thing you may have done; praying will always turn your energy around for the better.

Pray to, whomever, whatever or whenever you choose. Pray to the mountain, pray to ancestors, pray to the earth, pray to Tao(but it would not listen), pray to Jehovah, pray to the Great Mother, Allah, Buddha, Jesus, Lakshmi, Shiva, pray to the Great Spirit, it makes no difference. Praying is merely a device for realigning the mind, energy and passion of your local self with the mind, energy and passion of your universal self. When you pray, you are praying to the god or goddess within you. This has an effect on your energy field, which in turn translates into a positive charge that makes something good happen.

The lines above took us through the light thrown by religious philosophy on the subject of Love. Ideals in relationships are good to be kept in mind and they should form the foundation of interaction with the world around us. Pragmatic moderation would be necessary to live through the ups and downs of life with the passage of time.

PARENTING

The child must feel secure. Parents have to naturally start by giving. The child, as he or she grows looks forward to the demands being met, with asking or without asking for the same. There is the recognition on the part of the parents that the child is a body of one's own body and a soul from one's own. To feed is a pleasure, to clothe is another pleasure and to go out to acquaint with the world with accompanying family is another addition. All through the individuality of the child is accepted whole heartedly. There has to be a way to gain acceptance of the good and bad pointed out during the course.

The error of over indulgence or contrarily use of pressure to remain within stiff parameters can result in very untowardly rebellion soon after. A worse case is that, in society like ours in India, the antagonistic feelings or even hatred may keep on simmering over the years and may result in apathy or retaliation of some sort in the later years. The first symptom would be when the child does not like to study at school, the subjects advised by you. Furthermore, the liking of a profession or course of life would be of a different and independent choice. **In extreme cases,** the male or female teenager or youngster could fall a prey to bad company with the ills of smoking, drugs, remaining away from home, sexual promiscuity as retaliation against family rule. In conservative families, where children would be forced to live under fear of punishment all the time for smallest mistakes, cases are known of children forming unhealthy habits in a kind of perverse excitement.

If the child is not understood by the parents, he/she would join friends to explore sex. Energies of the child have to be kept engaged in sport or studies by eliciting the child's interest.

The bickering parents, if appearing to be moving towards breaking-up, shake the very foundations of security which they had built up earlier for the child. The confidence in being supported in time of need is damaged. The psychological moorings of the child with the security from the family get disturbed. A following consequence is the hardening attitudes of the child. The malleability of the personality recedes. Bickering parents shouting at each other are likely to be imitated by their children as they pick up the vocabulary and the gestures.

The social mores, customs, accepted systems and responses are different in different cultures of the east and west. However with the spread of western civilisation and education in English, globalisation on the media, World Wide Web, and facilities of communication, the responses of young generation are gaining uniformity already in the urban areas and spreading further geographically. Divorce, earlier unheard of in India is by now a commonly accepted mode of the ultimate solution to family discord. Live in relationships are now known as such in the cities. Common public is now aware of the legal acceptance accorded to same sex relationships as also the movements for power beyond emancipation to women.

From teenage onwards the Y generation asks for more independence than earlier times and manages to get it. Better it is for parents to give willingly and participate rather than yield grudgingly.

LOVE PRE-MARITAL AND EXTRA MARITAL

Carnal pleasures are abundantly available depending upon the resources of money and time that one has. It all depends on one's inclination. If one is married to one's ambition for achievement, time is likely to be scarce and inclination is likely to be missing for pleasure for pleasure's sake. My feeling is that a feeling of guilt, explicit or implicit, is hard to avoid in acts considered as immoral by the society. One night stands are in fashion where any future commitment or emotional involvement is hard to come by. Debauchery and fornication are more than likely to cause avoidable complications to life. Faithlessness to one's spouse has to be overcome by some specially devised means. Lucky are those whom nature has given qualifications and the intent to remain faithful to each other; this must result in a spiritual solace to the mind. Try and live for lasting peace of mind.

MARITAL LOVE

Well said that, do not try to eat a fruit before it is nurtured. If happiness is wanted, it has to be given as well. Mutual courtesies have to be shown, say, male chivalry and female grace, male has to gift a loving regard time and again and female's thankfulness thro' a look of the eyes, a smile or words of recognition are all very welcome. There is nothing more encouraging than an appreciation from one's spouse for an act of kindness, a job well done, or a situation handled appropriately. Many occasions arise, a few of them daily, quite some now and then and so many in a life time. Two wheels to a cart, is the saying in India, go through ups and downs of life in togetherness, in sober companionship, in unspoken unity of objective, with an emotional living together of life and its provisions granted by the Almighty.

Romance between a married couple, the thrill of the beginning, the nurturing in the middle age and the spiritual maturity of the declining years, is so full of variety and richness that it cannot be stored on a paper or any medium because it is so many things to the individuals, amenable only to experience, never adequately expressed. The male would better utilize all the faculties under his command to physically arouse love in the female and aim for her satisfaction prior to his own; in that case the vibrations of love would engulf both the partners. Physical love making is an art to be perfected as per one's own liking and capacity. It sustains marital happiness in joint efforts through the life-time and lasts beyond ageing.

Marital unhappiness is caused by selfishness in human nature which has to be kept aside in a getting together by holy matrimony. Resentment arises when one partner tries to impose oneself upon the other; this develops into a conflict of egos. No way, but to collect yourself and remember the vows to cooperate in all circumstances. The lesson has to be learnt, the hard way if necessary, any one of the two to act in humility and grant space to the other. For your own world not to come crashing down, the couple has to live in harmony and be wise enough to gauge the consequences.

MANAGING AN ORGANIZATION WITH LOVE

Reference is given to recognized definitions of Management, its functional aspects and the integral part played by Love to make a success of it all.

Management is a vital aspect of the economic life of man, which is an organized group activity. A central directing and controlling agency is inevitable for units of economic activity.

The productive resources viz. material, capital and labour etc. are entrusted to the organizing skill, administrative ability and enterprising initiative of the Management. Thus management provides leadership to a business entity. Without able managers and effective managerial leadership the resources of production remain merely resources and never become production. Under ever changing economy and environment the quality and performance of managers determine both the survival as well as progress of any enterprise. Management cadre enjoys such place of distinction in any nation that the welfare of its people and destiny of the country are under its influence.

Management is the process of getting things done through other people to achieve the pre-determined objectives of organization. The process by which given purpose of execution is put into operation and put to supervision. This is the function of executive leadership anywhere.

Management may also be defined as, "A technique by which the objectives and purpose of a particular human group are determined, defined, clarified and accomplished."

FROM BUSINESS POINT OF VIEW, management is the art of securing maximum results with the minimum of efforts so as to get maximum prosperity and benefit for both the employer and the employee (and as a matter of fact for all the stake holders) and give public the best possible service.

Management is a distinct process consisting of planning, organizing, staffing, leading and controlling, utilizing in each, both the science and art as also supervising the entire activity to achieve predetermined objectives of the organization.

Management starts at the empirical level by managing oneself. Most things are achieved in life if one could well manage the time available at one's disposal. Every one, whether educated or uneducated, an office executive or a farmer tilling the land possesses the uncanny human ability to manage one's own affairs in bipolar dimensions of his own self and of the universe of his concern.

This writer wishes to suggest in all humility that LOVE be treated as an undercurrent to all the activity listed above, love is a backdrop to the throbbing life just as your palpitating heart loves you otherwise how would life continue.

For anything to do well, start loving yourself if you are not doing that already. Look at every possibility, every means at your disposal to REMAIN HEALTHY, HAPPILY ALIVE AND KICKING. So many ways are there for a correct life-style, the means of naturopathy, and the field of alternative medicine available as a preventive measure, if one is already hale and hearty.

FUNCTIONS OF BUSINESS MANAGERS

Let us assume that PROFIT is the primary motive of business, otherwise how would there be capital multiplication or creation of reserves. Obviously, money is needed one way or another as soon as you step out to do any good. To get the money from the customer's pocket, the product or service has to be of utility to the customer. Without sincerity in attitude, this is not possible. The bond that exists is better to be handled with love.

PLANNING

Technicalities can well be handled by the engineers but the humane aspect has to be managed from the individual entrepreneurial level upward by the board of directors. As soon as the stages of planning kick off, recognition better be given side by side to the humane angle such as space and environment to work, comfort level necessary and the logistical support to get the best out of human effort and application of mind for work study plans to succeed.

Well begun is half done, goes the saying. Planning as the foremost activity in any business, applies foresight for creation, structure, functioning and control of an organization to achieve the identified objectives. If one does not keep in view the humane angles at each step how could the action materialize from human brain and hands for desired ends. Only love begets a loving reaction.

The objectives need to be specified in clear, unambiguous terms. They have to be practical, workable, achievable and ofcourse, acceptable. Wherever possible they need to be figuratively specified. Planning has to provide for economical and optimum usage of human, financial and material resources. As manager you are the representative of the supreme one so treat them all as your own to be of benefit to all of our own family, the stake holders, be it the promoters, your community, the shareholders, your country, the society in globalised relation placed anywhere geographically. **Planning involves** a consideration of likely events in future. The socio-economic conditions, the political picture, the macro and micro economic factors, are all relevant.

Derivative planning would need to provide for the adjustments required. In the course of choice to be made between alternative courses of action human needs would naturally condition the choice.

ORGANIZING

It is through an organization that synchronization of human, material and financial resources is planned and implemented. The participants are like the members of a team. The interpersonal relations at different levels have to be amicable enough to be mutually supportive. Activities have to be grouped and classified accordingly. Departmentalisation, creation of hierarchy, and classification of authority help in achieving efficiency in the running of an organization. Who is accountable to whom, as a principle makes the organization click.

For the sake of coordination between authority and responsibility, inter-personal relations have to be sustained on the basis of ethical interaction. Balance between politeness and straightforward communication begets correct understanding on the work platform. Stronger the links better is the communication in its genuineness and effectiveness as the information content flows up and down the chain. Ethics in dealings is an automatic prayer to the Supreme One for success and better results.

STAFFING

There are likely to be separate hierarchies for line and staff functions. In modern management, the two systems may overlap as per necessity and convenience of effectiveness.

Procurement, Storage, Production, Packaging, Marketing, Selling, Distribution, after Sales service and such other revenue generating systems are organized as line functions. Staff functions such as Public Relations, Human Relations (Staff), Accounting and maintenance support the line functions. Recruitment and placement requirements include defining and finalizing the job content, the range of skill requirements, induction process, remuneration, perquisites, and the gamut of policy clutch to retain employee loyalty for the organization.

LEADING/DIRECTING

More than influencing, leadership is about motivating a group to progress for achievement of objectives or goals. Organizations are usually over managed rather than appropriately motivated by their manager leaders. Possibly enhanced effort is needed to listen enough and counsel adequately.

Let us pay attention to the traits of leadership (where human approach is needed with a flavor of 'love' for the addressed ones) :-

IMPULSE (Drive)

The go-getter attitude, the backing of above average energy, initiative for their ambition.

MOTIVATION

Leaders are willingly assertive and in-charge of the situation. They have the capacity to gain and direct attention of their receptors for firm objectives.

ETHICS IN THOUGHT, SPEECH AND ACTION

Their honesty and integrity is not in doubt. Whatever is promised is delivered or impeccable effort is visible.

SELF CONFIDENCE

A leader has to be assertive and a decision-maker. Should have courage to admit mistakes and suitably atone for them. Balance has to be maintained between emotionality and enthusiasm.

COGNITIVE ABILITY

Not necessary to be a genius but level of intelligence, perception and ability to think strategically, the higher the better. The judgement to arrive at correct and timely concepts by a distinctive analytical ability and common sense is a requisite.

RELEVANT KNOWLEDGE

A leader has to be adept with the knowledgeability of the subject with which he is dealing, his aims and objectives, processes involved and the field of his operation. He is qualified accordingly.

A realization of the truth of this universe, the soul and the spirit would stand a leader in good stead in times of his test by opportunities.

CORPORATE SOCIAL RSPONSIBILITY

Describes itself when called corporate conscience, corporate citizenship, social performance, sustainable responsible business.

The principle is, give back a portion since so much has been received, A positive response is proposed to be given to, environment, consumers, employees, stakeholders and all members of the public who may be considered as stakeholders.

Business ethics is a form of applied ethics which follows the United Nations guide lines of Principles of Responsible Business Investment or ISO 26000, the recognized international standard for CSR. The concept is of corporate attitude towards housing, nourishment, social welfare, and environment etc. It is sought to improve upon this concept by way of help to build on the skills of local population as community based development is more akin to sustainable development. This thoughtfulness also encompasses the concept of better trade relationship with the marginalised producers and workers by giving them better equity. The principles involved are dialogue, transparency and respect for the value delivered by them.

Attention is also drawn to the concept of Environmental Management that exists to help the organizations (a) to minimise the adverse impact of their operations (processes etc.) on air, water and land, (b) to comply with local laws, regulations and other environmentally oriented requirements and (c) continually improve upon the aforesaid.

So much for the love of environment for the business as also our future generations. The depletion of ozone in the stratosphere should be matter of concern to all right thinking peoples of the world.

LOVE *A LA MODE* SPIRITUALITY

Life ought to be lived sportingly but virtuously. Keeping this in view I would like to draw upon the gems offered by a widely respected bank of Spirituality known the world over as **Srimad Bhagvad Gita**. To the best of my understanding the sayings of this scripture are generally endorsed by different religions in different words or ways and hardly negated as such.

Five thousand years ago or as some say, three thousand years ago there was a war in India on the plains known as Kurukshetra (believed to be in the province of Haryana where a city exists by that name) between the cousin brothers, five of them known as Pandavas (ethical ones led by the king Arjuna) and a hundred (sinful ones led by the king Duryodhana) on the opposite side. The latter did not want to yield a pin-head size of others' rightful land, was the cause of war among other reasons. Lord Krishna (an incarnation of God) sided with Arjuna and was his 'sarathi' (charioteer) of his five horse driven grand chariot.

While surveying the armies in mid-field, Arjuna became crest fallen and despondent upon facing the duty of killing his cousin brothers, family members and Gurus siding with Duryodhana for their personal reasons. There and then Lord Krishna gave him a sermon to treat his deficient mental disposition, this was transcribed into the treatise known as Gita by a Maharishi (Saint) named Vasudeva. Mahatma Gandhi treated this scripture as his most valuable guide. I choose to present the undernoted few Shlokas(verses in Sankrit, as translated into English by Sri Sri ParamhansYogananda) with my humble comments.

Verse 5 (Chapter III)
The Cosmic Lord said:

Verily, no one can stay for even a moment without working; all are compelled to perform actions willy-nilly, prodded by the qualities (Gunas) born of nature (Prakriti)

The universe is in continuous flux, in motion. Every living being is obliged to perform action, whether voluntarily or involuntarily. The body is pervaded with three 'gunas' (qualities) of nature. Called as Sattvic, Rajasik and Tamasik. These are applicable to tangible objects like actions and materials, as also they encompass the intangibles like thoughts and emotions. These are explained as follows, the content of Sattvic quality guides towards results that are moral, positive and uplifting. The direction of Tamasik quality is towards immoral, demeaning or negative. The Rajasik quality is neutral in that it is engaged more with the world, it is ego-centric, more material, has the positivities of pleasure and negativities of sorrow, has the potential to slide into into Sattvik or Tamasik patterns. Guru or the rightful thinking directs one towards Sattvik. Truthful and ethical lifestyle and possibly towards transcending levels of spirituality. The ultimate aim for the body is to evolve from worldly action into a realm of peace for the mind in the domain of super-consciousness and freedom from Karmic bondage.

Verse 8 (Chapter III)

Perform thou those actions that are obligatory, for action is better than inactivity, even simple maintenance of thy body would be impossible through inaction.

The Lord enjoins upon human beings to be absolutely sincere to the duties entrusted to them by the society.

Performances of these actions which may be as simple as that of a sanitary worker or as complicated as that of a scientist or a medical practitioner are equally valuable as a function of life. Consciousness of His companionship, His over-arching benevolent presence (the link of one's own soul to the Universal Soul, 'Param-atma') all through, is ordained. Such a relationship to the destined duties as they come your way would remedy the Karmic bondage with the world, which in turn is the basis for an opportunity to evolve in the next birth and beyond.

Inactivity even though practised by monks is looked down upon because the tendency to repay to the society in return for what all has been received is missing. A recluse is supposed to render service to the society by way of uplifting the general character and conduct of the community in addition to any others which may be enacted.

In the next verse the nature of Nishkama-karma (duties performed without a desire or attachment to expect favorable results) is explained as the desired conduct. This is apparently difficult to maintain but practically possible when recognized as the true path to tread upon.

Verse 9 (Chapter III)

Worldly people are Karmically bound by activities that differ from those performed as yajna (religious rites); O son of Kunti (Arjuna), **labour thou, unattached, in the spirit of yajna, offering actions as oblations.**

The religious rites performed in India from the times immemorial, of the times of Vedas, usually written in English as 'yajna' are actually pronounced in Sanskrit as YAGYA. The activity involves burning of fire in a sacred pit known as 'Hawan Kunda' and all the while to the accompaniment of chanting of 'mantras' offerings are made into the fire submitted to the almighty, intermittently with the pouring of pure Ghee (clarified butter) and scent emitting dry herbs etc. known as 'Samigri'. The whole activity has a very serene, ethereal kind of resonance. This activity is related to the Karma or duties enjoined upon oneself, in this verse.

People performing worldly duties with selfish motives, feelings of pleasure and pain, good or bad to each other, are intertwined with each other in obligations to be absolved in this life or next life. This is known as the Karmic bondage. Spirituality tries to resolve this conundrum.

Perform your duties with whatever ambitions or anxieties you may have, but (a) do not be intrinsically attached to the results because nothing is going with you at the time of final departure, (b) remember to mentally submit all your efforts, actions and contributions to the Almighty as humble offerings in a Yagya ceremony of life. Pleasure and pain are two sides of the same coin. Ideal is, to bear them with equanimity. If this appeal is fully comprehended, better to keep it to heart at all times.

At this juncture allow me to invite you to the next level of spirituality with the help of the following Shloka

Shloka-65 (Chapter XVIII)

Lord of the cosmos says,

> Manmanabhavmadbhakto, madyaji mam namaskuru,
> Maame-vaishyasiyuktyaiva,
> ma-aatmanam mat-parayanah.

Be my devotee mindfully. Control your mind (which is a most difficult thing to do). There is just one way to do it, practise, practise and practise.

Whatever actions you do (Try for Satvika, truthful, ethical), submit to me as your offerings in a Yagya (sacred fire) ceremony. You have a right and the duty to perform your designated Karma; you have no right or command over the result thereof.

Bow in 'Namaskar' to Myself.

Be-seated in Myself. See yourself in Myself. (Obviously, a realization of attachment to the Almighty).

Yoga, means in simple understanding 'plus' (i.e. sign of +). Attach yourself to Me, your soul to Super Soul of the universe.

THEN THOU SHALT BECOME ONE WITH ME.

I like to say to Dear Reader, remember Him whichever way you like, may He bless you!

JAI SHRI KRISHNA